Rwanda

A walk through darkness...
into light

Rwanda

A walk through darkness...
into light

Carl Lawrence

Gold Medallion author of "The Church in China"

VISION™
HOUSE
PUBLISHING, INC.

Gresham, Oregon 97030

RWANDA: A WALK THROUGH DARKNESS INTO THE LIGHT
© 1995 by Carl Lawrence

Published by Vision House Publishing, Inc.
1217 NE Burnside, Suite 403
Gresham, Oregon 97030

Printed in the United States of America

International Standard Book Number: 1-885305-34-6

Unless otherwise indicated, all Scripture references are from the Holy Bible: The New King James Version, © 1984 by Thomas Nelson, Inc.

95 96 97 98 99 00 01 02 03 04 - 10 9 8 7 6 5 4 3 2 1

Table of Contents

Part 1
A Walk through Darkness...

God is light
and in Him is no darkness at all.
If we say that we have fellowship with Him,
and walk in darkness,
we lie and do not practice the truth

(1 John 1:5b–6).

Introduction to Part 1

Why a book on Rwanda? Why should a nation with less than eight million people be the focus of so much attention?

After personally observing what happened there in April 1994, I was left with some haunting questions that needed answers.

Why is such a nation—professing to be 80 percent Christian and the beneficiary of two major revivals (1930s and 1970s)—tearing itself apart?

Are these Christians killing Christians?

On April 6, 1992, the slaughter began in Bosnia. Exactly two years later, April 6, 1994, it started in Rwanda. Can the cycle be broken?

Is this really a war of "ethnic cleansing" (i.e., racism), or is it another example of greedy, ambitious men using "ethnicity" as an excuse to grasp raw power?

Much of the information for this book was gathered from personal interviews done in Rwanda and surrounding refugee camps in April and May 1994, and during my return trip in April and May 1995. The interviews were less than satisfactory from a journalist's perspective because most of those interviewed did not want to be identified—by name or by details that might give away their identity. There are several reasons for this.

Most inhibiting is the fear factor. Tribal war has happened again and again and has never brought peace or resolution, but only set the stage for the next attack in a cycle of revenge. The survivors know the Hutu militia have, for the present, lost control of the country to the new Tutsi masters, the RPF, but the Hutu militia, disguised as refugees, have moved into the camps or into exile and are building a guerrilla army for the next round. Those interviewed do not want any documentation of their personal experiences or beliefs that may be used against them when the pendulum swings. They simply want to get back to their farms or villages or jobs and rebuild their lives with as little notoriety as possible.

They may suspect the interviewer of self-serving or of profit motives. Because of past events they have difficulty distinguishing between the motives of a plantation owner and a book publisher.

There was no animosity toward me, the interviewer, a stranger from a foreign land. But there was deep reluctance to trust anyone enough to share their identities or their emotions, so personal and painful and linked to memories almost too traumatic to relive.

An interviewer would be suspicious of anyone who said, "My name is so-and-so, and I want to tell you how those savage Hutus killed my family and what I think we should do about it!" The interviewer would suspect the person wanted to use him, and would have serious doubts about the person's credibility.

14

So, an interview often went something like this:

"You say everyone in your family was killed?"

"Yes."

"How many were in your family?"

Pause, a nervous shuffling begins.

"Four."

"Who where they?"

Another pause. "My wife...and three children."

"Three children. How old were they?"

All eye contact is lost at this point and usually never regained.

"Young children."

"How old were they?"

Answers with content were seldom or reluctantly given.

"How were they killed?"

"By the Hutu."

"How did they do it?"

Some interviews ended up being very short.

In agreement with the ground rules of these interviews, real names, occupations, or other identifying facts are rarely used. Basically the reference is to a "young husband" or some other nebulous term.

Don't let this take away from the validity of their testimony. They do have names. They are real people. They grieve as genuinely over the death of a loved one and over the rape of their country as much as does anyone in Los Angeles or Oklahoma City.

Rwandans may not weep or show emotions for the simple reason that there are no tears left. Though the tear ducts are empty, there will come a time for feeling—compassion, guilt, or anger.

But for now the soul's cry is, "No more. Not again. Not now!"

Rwanda: A Walk through Darkness

Give glory to the LORD your God before He causes darkness,
And before your feet stumble on the dark mountains,
And while you are looking for light,
He turns it into the shadow of death
And makes it dense darkness
(Jeremiah 13:16).

The darkness comes quickly, sometimes unmercifully, but always with inevitability, to the small Central African nation of Rwanda. The night shows no mercy to those who ignore its coming as they hurry about finishing tasks that must be done while there is still light.

Tension is thick as workers hurriedly move about stringing lights outside small restaurants so people can gather to talk, to laugh, but mostly to seek affirmation of

17

hope that this time the peace accord will hold and there will not be another war or massacre of innocent people.

Several assassinations of high-ranking officials have thrown a pall over the nation. The conversations are subdued. There is little laughter but there is hope. Their president is returning tonight from a peace conference in neighboring Tanzania. His plane, which also carries the president of the bordering country, Burundi, is due to arrive soon at the airport just miles away. Radios are tuned in as listeners wait for the classical music to be interrupted by an announcement that there has been a peace accord between the Hutus and Tutsis. The five hundred-year cycle of war will not be repeated. Rwanda will have come of age.

Sitting at one of the tables are two young women whose lives have intertwined. Uweri and Kayitesi have been friends for more than four years. Both are tall with finely chiseled faces that make them recognizably different from the Hutus. Both of them had come from a village, alone, to the city. They were like sisters. Their children played together, they attended the same church. During the days of Uweri's marital discord, which eventually led to separation and dissolution, Kayitesi's husband acted as a mediator. When that was no longer possible, he included Uweri's girls on picnics, outings, and sports events.

Kayitesi and her husband had recently taken their two children to school in neighboring Zaire. They told themselves it was because it had a much better educational system, but they both knew the real reason. Kayitesi had returned to Kigali for work while her husband stayed in Zaire to make some final arrangements.

At least three times a week Uweri and Kayitesi met at the market to talk, share experiences, and pray for each other. But tonight there was a weighty undercurrent at the restaurant, an underlying tenseness that pervaded the air.

It wasn't only at their table; it could be seen in the faces of the shorter, stocky Hutus who sat talking in serious tones at adjoining tables, while listening with one ear to a small radio beside them.

What none of those seated around the restaurant tables knew was that just off the end of the airport runway three men were hiding in the bushes—members of the president's elite guard. Later, a witness would testify that one of the three wore his beret a little differently than the other two and could have been a French mercenary. But there was no question about the stove-pipe type weapon that the foreigner had on his shoulder as he scanned the sky.

Uweri and Kayitesi stood to leave. They wanted to get home before it got any darker. As they stood, there was a sudden explosion and a flash of light in the sky, then darkness. Everyone stopped and stared. "What was that?" "It came from the airport." Silence made the suddenly darkened sky more ominous. A few miles away the French-built Mystere-Falcon jet carrying two presidents and their staffs catapulted toward the earth like a wounded bird with only one wing.

People turned their radios up—the classical music continued. Uweri and Kayitesi quickly hugged and hurried toward their buses to get home. They looked back, waved briefly, and went in opposite directions, self-consciously trying to act as if everything was normal and tomorrow they would laugh together over their "lack of faith."

Neither of them could know that as they hurried down the street they were taking the first steps of what would be—for themselves, their families, and millions of others—a walk through darkness.

Uweri sat quietly looking out the window of the bus as she headed for home. Her fellow passengers were unusually subdued. For three years she had made this same journey home from work, five nights a week, with many of these same people. They had become a bonded fraternity, swapping experiences, laughing, calling each other by name. The bus driver, instead of calling out a street name, would call the names of those who were to get off, adding a little quip. "Uweri, give the little ladies a hug for us all," was Uweri's signal to step off the bus and gather up her two daughters, six-year-old Elizabeth and eight-year-old Christina, who each night eagerly waited hand in hand beside the street. Together they would walk the block home, while talking, laughing, planning the evening, rehearsing the events of the day.

Umutomi, the lady who took care of the children in the daytime, had to leave a half hour before Uweri's bus arrived at her stop, but Uweri never worried. It was a safe neighborhood. People looked out for each other, especially after her separation from her husband. Several ladies became "Auntie" to the children.

But tonight, something was different. She had felt it as she and her friend, Kayitesi separated, calling out, "Until tomorrow." A heaviness had settled over her mind as she took her seat by the bus window. It was a feeling seemingly shared by those on board. She was shaken to realize that mentally she was noticing which passengers were Tutsi and which were Hutu. She hated that. She had taught her children that it didn't matter. She told them, "We are Christian and in Christ we are all brothers and sisters." She had heard Christina repeat that to her friends when rebuking them for slurs against the Hutus. Tonight there was no laughing or joking, only a silence filled with unanswered questions. "Will there be another war?" "Was that the president's plane that exploded?"

Uweri was startled when the lady beside her touched her on the arm. It was their first exchange in the twenty-minute ride.

"You're home...this is where you get off." The bus driver had simply called the street name. Everyone noticed. Uweri smiled at the driver as she made her way off the bus. He turned away. *He is a Hutu. He is probably ashamed,* she told herself. She had never even allowed herself to think that way before. What was wrong with her? The momentary guilt gave way to a powerful premonition as the door shut behind her and the bus pulled out into the traffic. She noticed that some passengers still looked at her through the window.

She stood alone. Her girls were not there. She looked down the street toward the house. Nothing. She told herself, "I must have spent more time than usual with Kayitesi. They were here and went home to wait." She looked at her watch. She was on time. She told herself not to panic; there was a reasonable explanation. She started a controlled walk toward the house. She wanted to run, but she knew that people would notice. The girls had probably told her Umutomi was staying late tonight.

The street was deserted. No children were out playing. She was nearly running. She didn't care who saw her—something was wrong! As she went by her neighbor's house she heard the front door slam shut.

Arriving at her own house she ran up the steps, took out the keys to unlock the door, and noticed the door was slightly ajar.

Taken aback, she looked at it for a second and slowly pushed it open, calling, "Girls, girls!" Cautiously, she looked into the shadowy room, "It's Mommy. Come on, let's get supper." No response. She dropped her purse and ran to their bedroom. Empty. The beds were made, the clothes picked up, but their favorite dolls that were always on the beds were gone. *Something is wrong. Oh, God, where are my girls?*

She ran to the back door. *They are probably out there playing house with their dolls, and have forgotten what time it is.* She opened it knowing they never played back there, but it was her last hope. For three years she had been attempting to get the neighborhood garbage dump moved from her back yard to someplace else. She had never succeeded. A black dog, rummaging through the garbage, looked up at her as if she were intruding on his evening meal, then went back to his supper.

Realizing the house was dark, she rushed from one room to another, turning on the lights, calling, " Elizabeth! Christina!"

She had no telephone. It was one of the conveniences that had to be given up after her marriage failed. She turned on the radio. Classical music was all she heard.

A note, of course, a note. She went to the living room and picked up the note pad they often used for messages. It was blank.

She forced herself to sit down. *Don't panic. I'm sure there is a rational reason. Oh, God, help me. Tell me, did we plan something for the girls that I have forgotten about? Please remind me.*

Silence. If there was such a plan God had forgotten about it too.

Her neighbors. *He's a Hutu and she's a Tutsi.* She was angry with herself. She had never thought of them in those terms before. Why now? She prided herself on not caring about or noticing anyone's tribe.

Running out her front door, she stopped for a second, composed herself, and—using every ounce of will power she possessed to hold back her anxiety—she walked to the neighbor's front door and knocked. No response. She knocked again. She had heard the door slam earlier so she knew someone was home. Still no response. She had knocked on the door hundreds of times before.

She knocked louder. A hidden voice quietly called out, "Who is it?"

"It's me, Uweri." This had never happened before. In times past the door would have been opened immediately and she would have been invited in.

"I'm looking for the girls. Do you know where they are?"

"I saw them leave about an hour ago with Umutomi. That is all I know, now please leave."

She stood in disbelief. Relief that the girls were safe didn't alleviate the surprise at her reception from one of her best friends.

A man's voice came through the door. "Go away, you will get us all into trouble." The door opened just a crack. A woman's voice filtered through, "Uweri, go home. Lock your door and turn your lights out." A man's voice cursed and the door was slammed shut.

Umutomi had taken the children home with her. But

why? What was happening? *I'll go find them.* She felt so alone and confused. This was one of those times when she wished she and her husband had tried a little harder. Maybe if she had had a little more patience, together they could have cured his illness.

Walking in the house, she turned on the radio just in time to hear the words that filled her with an unfamiliar foreboding. "The president has been murdered by Tutsi extremists. They have killed our president." The electricity went off and so did the radio—with those words still in the air. Uweri sat in total darkness, surrounded by fear.

Generation to Generation

Our fathers sinned and are no more,
But we bear their iniquities
(Lamentations 5:7).

Lush green mountains sloping into gentle hills of splendid grass, peaceful blue skies dotted with a continuous supply of moving cumulus, belie the fact that Rwanda is a divided country. This small nation of less than eight million people has been, and still is, divided by more than the famous Congo and Nile drainage system. It is divided by hate.

That omnipresent division is defined by two words: Hutu and Tutsi. One's tribal identification[1] is the first entry on the required identity card, and the designation will establish or affect each boundary of life—which schools are attended, salary limits, even potential marriage partners. It is the caste system personified.[2]

If your ID card says "Tutsi," you are part of a minority making up 14 percent of the population. People call you "tall one." Standing among the men of your tribe, a basketball recruiter would think he was in paradise. As a Tutsi your complexion is lighter than a Hutu's and your finely chiseled face resembles an Ethiopian. You are known as part of a pastoral people who, according to folklore, were cattle breeders who came from the Horn of Africa about five hundred years ago. Though your tribe is in the minority, you have been for many of those years the dominant caste holding the Hutu majority under a feudal system, with the power base being your cattle holdings. You are considered the Rockefellers of your society, the feudal elite. The cattle and land are your bank account. Until recently your tribe paid allegiance to a monarchy, a king.

If the word "Hutu" is printed on that ID card, you are part of a majority of 84 percent. Your stocky features suit you for rugby better than for basketball. You are known as a farmer, more docile, less aggressive than the cattle ranchers. Your people have experienced many years of domination by the minority Tutsis that has built up to an angry cry of "no more!"

Whether a Hutu or a Tutsi, you both remember the history of your ancestor's astonishment when in 1894 they first encountered a man with blonde hair, a red face, and a big nose: Count van Goetzen from Germany. Rwanda would never be the same. Following van Goetzen came men that would be described as: "...an odd group of individuals.... They do not look like the others though they are red. They do not have feet; they walk on bandages.

They see through things that shine and hide their eyes. There is always a cover on their heads. We do not know what to make of it."

Those first "white fathers" were followed by others in 1907 who "looked the same but did not cover their heads." The first missionaries had arrived, both Catholic and Protestant.

The inevitable happened. Colonialism came to Rwanda, and the king submitted to a German protectorate. Then the "protectors from that far away land," the Germans, lost a "great war somewhere," known as World War I. The newly formed League of Nations, considered by some an awkward "caste" of its own, turned Rwanda over to different red-faced men, Belgians, who were already occupying the Belgian Congo, now known as Zaire.

After another "great war," World War II, the United Nations, another clumsy "caste," decreed Rwanda a UN Trust territory still under Belgian rule. The Belgians, foreseeing how the winds of change were disfiguring colonialism, introduced and encouraged "democratic political institutions" while professing benevolence. The Tutsis saw this transfer of power as a threat to their monarchy. The Hutus saw it as an opportunity to lay claim to the justified rights of a majority tribe. The Belgians saw it as a graceful way to escape the horns of a dilemma and return to Europe. They ignored the Tutsi monarchy and handed the reins of government over to the Hutus.

In 1959 the Hutus sparked the first of many revolts. The Tutsi monarchy, like colonialism, was soon in the ash bin of history. Thousands died and 160,000 Tutsis fled to neighboring countries. This was the first of several exercises in "modern nation building." The exiles would not return to their land, but their children would—with an angry vengeance.

There was a UN supervised election. Rwandans didn't have much to say about it, but they were allowed to vote. With "one man, one vote," the Hutus won a "resounding victory." The UN, not wanting to be taken hostage by long-standing ethnic antagonism, terminated the Belgian Trusteeship and granted full independence to Rwanda and its brother neighbor, Burundi. Rwanda's new flag began to fly on July 1, 1962, under a Hutu-dominated government.

The election introduced a semblance of "democratic rule" with African variations. A duly elected president was placed in office, Gregorig Kayibanda. Like most emerging African nations, Rwanda was plagued by governmental inefficiency and corruption. On July 5, 1973, Kayibanda was supplanted by a military coup led by Major General Juvenal Habyarimana.

Habyarimana was raised in a society where his people, the Hutus, though numerically a majority, were at best third-class citizens. During his youth he had remained at the bottom of a caste system where ethnicity determined the course of daily life. For the ambitious young Hutu there was nowhere to go but up. Habyarimana went to Zaire for his education and when he returned he saw a changed Rwanda. His people, the "rightful rulers," were now in control and he was welcomed back. Habyarimana enrolled in the Army officer training school. His career was something akin to a meteor. By the age of thirty-six he was not only a major general, but he was leading a "bloodless coup." The blood would come later.

Like so many before him, he promised total equality between tribes and the end of political corruption. He appointed his best friend, Theoneste Bagosora, cabinet chief for the ministry of defense. He also filled many other key positions with his fellow tribesmen. A Hutu government was firmly in control.

Almost overnight, the Hutu leaders lost their two main excuses for not yet succeeding as a nation. One, the cold war ended. Two, the two super powers, one of whom was always the problem and the other the answer, were now absent from the equation. The ruling Hutus were no longer in a position to play one side against the other, siding with whoever offered the biggest Swiss bank account or the most modern weaponry.

The weakening world economy, plus the agitation by the RPF and militant Hutus spelled the beginning of the end for Habyarimana's regime, and set the final stage for the massacres that would follow after his death.

The sons and daughters of the Tutsis were in exile in Uganda waiting for this moment. Adopting the title of Rwanda Patriotic Front (the RPF), they invaded the hills of northern Rwanda from bases in Uganda. There were retaliation massacres against the Tutsis. The president was silent, but his defense minister and radio were not. The citizens were told in most unsubtle terms that "all Tutsis must die" and—like Herod of old—announced that "all Tutsi babies must be killed, as well, because the Tutsis attacking Rwanda today left here as little children." The premise was: Had we killed them then, we wouldn't have to kill them now.

Habyarimana was becoming desperate. He formed an elite group called the Presidential Guard. They were hand-picked extremists, well trained by very accommodating French mercenaries.

In 1991, Habyarimana personally contributed $200,000 to finance a military unit composed of recruited misfits of society. He called them *Interahamwe*, which means "those who kill as one." Habyarimana would realize too late that they would more than live up to their motto. The organization, with his blessing, soon became a home for a nationwide "boys-club-cum-death-club." Leaders were given distinctive tailor-made uniforms. Like the youth of Adolph Hitler and Mao's Red Guard, they strutted through small villages looking for recruits. The disgruntled rabble was trained not to defend Hutus but to kill Tutsis. They were sent out with machetes to kill sheep to practice for the massacring of Tutsis. They would later prove what good students they were.

Habyarimana's friend and defense chief, now Colonel Ranzaho, ordered that a census be taken. Somehow this sounds like history repeating itself. Houses in Kigali, the capital city, were marked with a special code, the meaning of which was made known only to the "militia," an amalgamation of the elite Presidential Guard and the Interahamwe. The "militia" became a word that would strike fear in all of Rwanda. People did not know that the mark on the entrance to their house was a symbol that determined whether or not that house would be passed over on a soon-to-come, fateful night.

While Habyarimana was in power, he and his close followers were known as the *Akazu*. In the language shared by the Hutus and Tutsis, Kinyarwanda, *Akazu* was used to describe "a little hut to which few can gain entry." In later years, a close member of the president's family said, "It came to describe a leper's house, a place where one could be killed merely by coming into contact with the people inside."

At 8:05 P.M. on April 6, 1994, racial hatred, terror, and corruption burst into flame over the lush gardens surrounding the Kigali Airport. Before the president's body hit the ground, the darkness from the heat-seeking missile had triggered what would become one of the worst massacres in modern history.

1 Rwandans from small minority tribes (less than 1 percent of the population) sometimes designate themselves as one of the majority groups in order to fit within the mainstream of society.

2 Note: This chapter contains a brief review of Rwandan history. However, it would be inaccurate to evaluate President Habyarimana's leadership from 1973 to April 1994 by what happened after his assassination. He had been considered a moderate leader who gave Rwanda considerable freedom and, by African standards, a near democracy. Under his leadership, roads were built, improving availability of food supplies, health and education systems were developed and the standard of living was improved. Responsibility for what happened after April 1994 might better be placed at the door of militant Hutus in Habyarimana's government, and the Tutsi army-in-exile, the Rwandan Patriotic Front (RPF).

Sitting in the silent darkness, Uweri tried to picture her children. If they were here, they would quickly cuddle up to her with a smile, and Christina would say, "Don't worry, Mommie. God is holding our hand. He will take care of us." The difference between them was that her daughter really believed that was true.

She picked up her purse to go to Umotomi's to collect the girls, but the sound of screeching tires and shouting stopped her short. Going to a window, she carefully held the curtain back just far enough to see outside.

Oh, God, what is happening?

Her house sat on a knoll with the street leading down into a main traffic artery. She could see a jeep being parked across the main road, creating a roadblock. Several young men jumped out and stood with AK–47s poised, ready to fire. One took his machete and ran to the side of the road, chopping large branches from the trees. Another dragged the branches across the road, making the roadblock complete. She was trapped.

As Uweri moved back from the window she heard the first staccatos of machine gun fire that would violate not just her street but, in the days to come, all of Rwanda.

She became physically ill as she heard a woman cry out, "Merci, merci." Young men gleefully shouted, "I got me a cockroach, I got me a cockroach." She knew what they meant.

She rushed through darkness into the kitchen and

pulled a candle out of a drawer. Lighting it, she cupped the flame with her hands to reveal as little light as possible. Digging into her purse, she pulled out her wallet and took out her plastic-covered ID card. Holding it close to the candle she looked at that first entry: "Tutsi." Her death warrant.

I have to get rid of this, she thought.

She peered about in the darkness. Stepping to a book shelf, she pulled out a book and tucked the small ID card inside, then placed the book back on the shelf. Retrieving the candle, she headed for her bedroom. Opening the dresser's bottom drawer, she found the box containing all her valuable papers—her own and her daughters' birth certificates, her marriage license. She unfolded a piece of paper she had brought from her village when she came to Kigali as a young woman seeking a career. The ethnic designation listed on it was the small tribe into which she was born. The fateful words *Tutsi* or *Hutu* were not named because at that time she had not yet chosen to identify herself with the Tutsis, in order to have a career. If she used this paper as her ID maybe it would be believed that she was neither Hutu nor Tutsi. A moment of shame came over her at her cowardice at being aligned with those who were under attack, but her survival instinct caused her to refold the paper and tuck it down the front of her dress.

Raucous laughter and shouts of "Kill the Tutsis" moved from the roadblock up her street. They were coming. She had to hide. She blew out her candle. She was down on her knees, ready to crawl under the bed when she realized the predictability of being found there. There was no place to hide. She ran to the back door. She would make a run for it. No, there was no place to run.

Suddenly, she remembered a narrow crawlspace between the kitchen ceiling and the tin roof of the house. It was where her former husband used to store his bottle of "medicine." There was a small sliding panel just above the kitchen table. On more than one night she had heard him wrestle with the panel, frustrated until he reached his cache. She would cry herself to sleep knowing that in the morning she would find him at the table, asleep, with an empty "medicine" bottle by his side.

Could she fit into the space? How big was it? The shouts, the gunfire, gave her little time to argue with herself. She ran to the kitchen, falling over a chair. Lying on the floor, she looked up, trying to see the square panel, just above the table. She took off her shoes before realizing she wasn't going to worry about getting the table dirty. Climbing up on the table, she pushed the panel up and aside. Stifling heat generated by the sun on the tin roof hit her in the face. There was no other choice. Standing on tip toes she stuck her head in the pitch dark space. Would it hold her? Should she try it?

A burst of gun fire answered her question. She grabbed the frame with both hands and tried to pull herself up. She didn't have the strength. Maybe she could put a chair on top of the table. Pounding at the front door changed her mind. With one adrenaline-laden pull, her chest scraped across the frame as she made another desperate attempt. Her head hit the metal roof, pulling her feet in behind her, she quickly slid the panel back into place.

As she did, she heard a crash at the front door, and shouts in her living room. "We know you're here, Tutsi. Come on out, let's have a party. Your neighbors said you were here, so come on. We'll find you."

She was afraid to breath. Caught in a contorted position, partly on her chest and partly on her side, barely balanced on the widely spaced rafters, she dared not move. Heat and fear were suffocating her.

She heard her home being torn apart, sounds of glass being smashed, furniture being broken, interspersed with cursing. She stopped breathing. They were in the kitchen. At the kitchen table. Right below her. *Oh, God, don't let them look up! Did I leave a shoe behind?* She wiggled her toes. No, both shoes were on her feet.

She heard cupboard doors being opened. They were eating her food. Sitting at her table. Right below her. One sound from her and a bullet through the ceiling would end her life.

She could hear them boasting about their evening's killings and their eagerness for her to show up at the house. She was paralyzed with fright. Her legs grew numb. *Oh, Lord, don't let me sneeze...or itch...or move...*

Her sanctuary exploded as a spray of bullets came through the ceiling and ricocheted off the metal roof. The only hit was her left cheek where a spent bullet landed.

Silently she wept, thinking of her children. *Oh, my little girls, where are you now? Are you safe?*

Chairs noisily scraped across the tile floor before the strident noises began to subside. From outside the house came occasional voices, accentuated by the rattling sound of gunfire and intermittent screams as machetes were used to save bullets. One sound merged with another. The hours passed as Uweri spent her first night as a prisoner of war in her own country.

The Massacre

Yet hear the word of the LORD, O women,
And let your ear receive the word of His mouth;
Teach your daughters wailing,
And everyone her neighbor a lamentation.
For death has come through our windows,
Has entered our palaces,
To kill off the children—no longer to be outside!
And the young men—no longer on the streets!
Speak, "Thus says the LORD:
'Even the carcasses of men shall fall
as refuse on the open field,
Like cuttings after the harvester,
And no one shall gather them' "
(Jeremiah 9:20–22).

If one definition of darkness is a place where God does not reside, then the word "darkness" is aptly used to describe the 110-day war that began in Rwanda on April 6, 1994. After hearing what happened the first night of the massacres one wants to stop and say, "Okay! I get the point! Can we move on?" We can't. As painful as it may be to read about what took place, we need to see and hear Hutus and Tutsis as they, more often than not reluctantly and humbly, attempt to unravel their personal tragedies.

The lamentations of the prophet Jeremiah give voice to their grief and pain:

> I am the man who has seen affliction by the rod of His wrath. He has led me and made me walk in darkness and not in light.
>
> He has set me in dark places like the dead of long ago. He has hedged me in so that I cannot get out; He has made my chain heavy. Even when I cry and shout, He shuts out my prayer.
>
> You have covered Yourself with anger and pursued us;
>
> You have slain and not pitied. You have covered Yourself with a cloud, that prayer should not pass through.
>
> You have made us an offscouring and refuse in the midst of the peoples. All our enemies have opened their mouths against us. Fear and a snare have come upon us, desolation and destruction.
>
> O LORD, You have seen how I am wronged; judge my case. You have seen all their vengeance, and their schemes against me. (Lamentations 3:1–2, 6–8, 43–47, 59–60)

Their story is a modern litany of carnage, recited by a suffering nation.

* * *

The president's plane crashing into the bushes seemed, in retrospect, to signal the execution of a well-orchestrated plan to "cleanse the Rwandan government of all opposition" (i.e., Tutsis). Within the hour, the nation, especially the capital city, Kigali, was reeling out of control. The gates of hell were opened and the devils were loosed.

Moments after the explosion of light in the sky, people sensed something terrible had occurred. They quickly left the marketplace and headed for home, their families, and what they mistakenly thought would be safety. For many, their home would be a place of death for them and all who lived there.

Before hearing the official announcement on the radio of the president's murder, the prime minister was disturbed by a group of young men pounding on her front gate, demanding entrance. The guards refused to open the tall metal structure. This was one of the houses that had been marked by the census takers. As the gate was being bashed open the prime minister ran to a neighbor's house for safety. Relentlessly, the gang came, moving from one house to another, smashing gates, threatening occupants, killing, spraying the house with bullets so no one could hide. Then there was a scream, a cry for mercy, and the prime minister lay dead as the gang of "militia" turned and went to another home that had the damning mark. The process was repeated again and again. The militia was joined by others—many good citizens—wanting to be on the "right" side.

Roadblocks suddenly appeared on the streets. Cars were stopped as the "militia" ordered everyone out. If your ID card said you were a Tutsi, or you were known as a moderate Hutu, there was no time for explanation or a plea for mercy. The machetes would come down and you would be hacked to death while a driver was either ordered to move on or the car was sprayed by AK–47s.

Ten young men called their commander on military radios and asked what to do. They were ordered back to their barracks and were told not to shoot and to give up their arms. They did. Moments later the "militia" showed how well they had learned to handle their machetes. They first hacked the Achilles tendons of the ten young men. Then, as the they lay writhing on the ground, unable to stand, they hacked them to pieces. There was a moment of celebration before the militia moved on, leaving behind the slashed and bleeding remains of the dead Belgian soldiers from the UN peacekeeping force.

The president's death was announced on the radio. Later, the same station would air shouts of encouragement to the militia. "Kill the Tutsis; all Tutsis must die." To the Tutsis, the Hutu militants shouted, "You cockroaches, you are made of flesh. We won't let you kill us. We will kill you first." And they did, indiscriminately, with animal intensity.

Before morning came, any organization or discipline had evaporated in the wild euphoric melee of the sound of the machete dissecting flesh, the stuttering fire of AK–47s and the occasional blast of hand grenades.

Those houses that had been marked by the censors had been taken care of and now anyone was fair game. The mobs moved into different parts of the city. Parents huddled with their children, but for many it was too late. The sound of smashing doors, screams, and then the silence of death moved from house to house.

A young husband gathered his wife and child and ran down the street to the house of his supervisor. It was dark and they were greeted by a smashed door. They couldn't see in the darkness that enveloped them, but they sensed by the silence that this house had already been visited, and not by an angel of mercy. The family lay on the floor, huddled together in the hallway. After several hours, the young man crawled toward the living room and stared through the darkness at what appeared to be several piles of clothes in the living room. As morning light came, he realized the clothes were covered with blood, the death shrouds of the father, mother, and three children—one less than four months old. Why they were killed he would never know for they were Hutus, killed by Hutus.

Dawn brought no relief, only a change in strategy.

He crawled back to his wife and child. They decided to move to the church, less than a block away. Churches had always been safe before. Like thousands of others, they believed even the militia would not attack the house of God. Clutching their child, they stood to leave when they heard a voice. They fell back to the floor. Listening intently, they agreed it was the sound of someone approaching with a loudspeaker. As it drew closer to the house they understood the words, "Go...stadium...you will be safe."

Huddling together, they cautiously moved to what used to be the front door. They could hear the shuffle of some-one passing the house. They stood quietly, holding their sleeping child, then moved a few feet further and saw other people going by the house. Some were weeping. All were fearful; all moving as one down the street.

The distance to the stadium was a two hour walk. As they trekked through the streets, there were no words to explain what they saw. Bodies in various death poses lay across the streets. Cars were sprayed with bullet. Bodies were hanging out of windows.

Surly militia manned roadblocks, but paid little attention to the crowd of people heading for the stadium. No one dared make eye contact with them. No one spoke. Fear and shock allowed no display of emotion or even recognition, except the gravitation together of those who knew each other.

Trucks drove by loaded with disfigured bodies. Though thousands of Tutsis were moving toward the stadium, people were afraid to look up, even at the sound of machine gun fire or a scream. The militia would suddenly walk up to a group, point to someone ordering them out of the line. The rest huddled tightly together but continued walking, trying to blank out the sounds of pleas for mercy before the one chosen was hacked down like a tree.

At last the stadium and refuge were in sight. They had been assured that there they would be safe.

The young husband had attended many sporting events there. He had cheered wildly for his team; had enjoyed the camaraderie of his friends. He always liked the view from section six.

As he, with thousands of others, entered the stadium he saw the field was nearly filled with people sitting or lying—some who had apparently been there for hours. All were waiting to be rescued from this nightmare.

The young husband tried to lead his wife toward section six, but he could see it was already full of people so he stayed where he was. Suddenly, an explosion! A mortar shot from outside landed indiscriminately inside the stadium. There were screams of terror from survivors and cries of agony from the dying. Everyone fell to the ground. As he cautiously looked up he could see section six strewn with bodies. People were trying to move from one section to another. Another mortar landed...section ten...then section four. People now realized this was not a place of safety, but a death trap. They had been herded here so they could be killed. Children were left behind as people ran for the exits, trampling each other to death. From somewhere the mortars continued their barrage. Screaming people ran in panic in all directions. They now thought of the one historically safe place to run: a church.

In the past, when fighting broke out, they were always privileged sanctuaries. People stayed there for days until the fighting died down. Then they would either go into exile in another country or return to their home or some other place of safety.

This time things were different. There would be no sanctuary.

A church that usually held two hundred was packed with twice that number. There was a hush except for an occasional baby's cry and desperately whispered prayers. Even that was quiet when loud pounding was heard at the gates. "Open up, we want to come in." The pastor shouted back that this was God's house and the people inside were under God's protection. "Go away."

Several more shouts. "Send out the men and you can keep the women and children." Still no response.

"Send out the women and children. You can keep the men." The whispered prayers began again with more fervor.

The gate was smashed. The front door was kicked off its hinges and a tear gas grenade was lobbed into the middle of the sanctuary. People ran for the exit. Another grenade exploded.

In a few minutes, people stood huddled in the church yard with faces streaked with tears, coughing.

Flatbed trucks pulled up and the people were ordered to get on. They would be taken to safety. Any reluctance was met by an AK–47 thrust into a shivering body.

Parents lifted their children on board and then crawled up themselves. The pastor was told to say behind. He was a Hutu. As the truck pulled away the pastor heard screams, gun shots, hacking of bones and raw flesh. Later, when he attempted to drive away, the road was blocked by bodies that had been thrown from the trucks. A couple of blocks away he saw the empty trucks. Four hundred who had sought refuge in God's house now lay strewn out like a Picasso sculpture of death. The pastor knelt and prayed over what had been his congregation.

This scene was repeated in church after church. Only for some there were no trucks. The "militia" would simply burst through the door, toss grenades or spray the place with machine gun fire. They then stepped on and over the bodies and if anyone moved they were slashed with a machete.

In the cities, stadiums and churches became death traps, so the people headed for the countryside. They started out in small groups that grew as others joined them. As they would come to a clearing, the militia would materialize suddenly.

Later, a "young pastor" reluctantly told of the carnage. Just days before the massacres he heard the Lord call his name and tell him "something terrible is going to happen. People will come against your village. They will have spears and guns and they will kill everyone. You will survive, but all of your family will be killed." At the time he dismissed the words as a bad dream. Now he realizes they were much more than that. They were a living nightmare.

Two hundred militia came to his village. Over twenty thousand people had gathered there for safety. The militia saw the odds and left. More than half of those gathered left for the bushes, hoping to eventually find refuge. The young pastor decided to stay. The militia came back, this time with fifty more men. First they moved everyone to a clearing, then led the women and children away, saying they would be given food. The men remained behind. Without warning, grenades were thrown into their midst, exploding, tearing apart, maiming, killing. Then the AK–47s did their work and finally the militia moved over the bodies with their machetes.

The young pastor, partially covered by two bodies and soaked in their blood, lay still, afraid to breath. He could hear the militia laughing, "Here's one we didn't get. Death to you, Tutsi!" Then the sound of a machete into a skull. They stood over him and there was silence. He waited for the machete to come crashing down. They moved on. He took a silent breath and lay very still. For awhile it was quiet and then the sounds of death and rape filled the air.

His family of nine were all dead. A burial party estimated there were nine thousand bodies, yet the young pastor had survived. He now tries to pray but can only cry, "God, how could you let this happen? Why?" He wrestles with unbelief. Many times he had told his congregation, "Just believe in God and He will take care of you." Now he is uncertain.

The militia, young rebels like Mao's Red Guard in China and Pol Pot's Khmer Rouge in Cambodia, did not destroy without official encouragement.

Hours after the president's death a new cabinet had been formed. Eliezer Niyitigeka was appointed as minister of information. He had studied journalism at a university in Romania, but was thrown out of that country when he stabbed and killed a fellow student.

He had returned to Rwanda and become a ranking official. He had others that would do his killing for him now. He returned to his home province where, according to the city mayor, he encouraged the militia to continue the massacre. "He did not say directly, 'Kill Tutsis,'" reports the mayor, but rather, he would couch his words in terms the militia would understand: "You are doing a good job. Don't stop now." The only job many of them ever had was killing Tutsis and he knew it. When he urged the militia, now joined by local Hutus who didn't want to be caught on the wrong side, that "now would be a good time to clear the bushes," it was a signal for the militia and their new recruits to go outside the city and kill any Tutsis that were still hiding there. That job done, they returned to the city and he would congratulate them on doing their job so well and suggest, "Now would be a good time to clean around their houses." This launched a new search for any Tutsi hiding near their home. The enthusiastic search began and more Tutsis died. The ranks of the militia grew as respectable citizens joined their ranks. Neutrality was not permitted.

Thanks to the minister of information, churches and stadiums in Kibuye became killing grounds, with almost ten thousand massacred. Good Samaritans took some of the injured to a hospital. The militia followed and one by one killed the bandaged survivors.

The atrocities continued...and continued...and continued. The rivers flowed with bodies. First to be seen were the men, dismembered. The militia had hacked off the legs of the much taller Tutsis, then thrown the men who were crying for mercy into the river to swim, shouting, "Now we've brought you down to our size."

Then came the bodies of the women, hacked by machetes. Finally the children, thrown into the river while still alive. No use wasting ammunition or time on those who would drown anyway.

After a couple of days the rivers were literally blocked with bodies. Lake Victoria was polluted and newspapers around the world began to print stories, unread by many, that "thirty-six thousand were buried in one mass grave." Similar stories followed for months. Parts of Lake Victoria are still polluted.

Some of the bodies were dead from neat little holes in their heads. The "militia" gave some a choice. You could buy from them a bullet and they would kill you quickly with it, but if you did not have the money, you had no choice but to be hacked to death with a machete, free.

Gary Haugen, a United Nations genocide investigator visited some of the sites. His observation, written for *Christianity Today*[1] ten months later, puts in words what others saw first hand.

> The most difficult part of the job for me was not so much examining the carnage but interviewing the survivors. I sorted through thousands of lacerated and crushed skulls and bore the stench of mass graves containing the fleshy remains of thousands of naked children, mothers, brothers and grandfathers. But that was not as painful as holding eye contact with a survivor as she described how she hid for two-and-a-half days among the corpses and severed limbs after a massacre. Or listening to a man tell

how he crawled among the dead for three days on the cathedral floor, wounded and desperately thirsty, nearly smothering a surviving child who wanted to cry out when the murderers returned to beat more survivors to death.

Narrating what became a familiar pattern, one survivor, a fourteen-year-old girl with pink machete scars across the back of her neck, told how she fled to the local church with the other Tutsi when the killing began. When the local Hutu mob could not overcome the church's defenses, government soldiers cleared away the Tutsi resistance. With hundreds of defenseless women and children before them, the butchers were free to do their work.

The sanctuary had been filled to capacity, with the dead piled in blood-soaked heaps, limbs and heads scattered. In this church the blood line staining the walls is knee-high.

We visited church upon church where the dead lay frozen in their last moment of terror, or where bulldozers had to be used to find the true dimensions of the church's mass grave. I learned the slaughter was not the work of a few crazed men. It had been done by countless ordinary individuals—a school principal, a farmer, a merchant, a doctor, a magistrate.

While this was happening, another Army—the exiled Tutsi RPF, better trained and disciplined than the roving mobs of militia—were steadily moving south from Uganda, their place of exile. Meanwhile, the Hutu militia and civilian sympathizers who had participated in the massacres discarded their uniforms and their weapons and inconspicuously joined the hundreds of thousands of women and children fleeing the militia for what would turn out to be massive refugee camps, where the suffering would continue and they would attempt to regroup.

They tracked our steps so that we could not walk in our streets. Our end was near; our days were over, for our end had come. Our pursuers were swifter than the eagles of the heavens. They pursued us on the mountains and lay in wait for us in the wilderness. (Lamentations 4:18–19)

1 Gary Haugen, *Christianity Today*, 6 February 1995, 52–54.

Uweri woke with a start. Trying to gather her thoughts, she closed her eyes. Where was she? What was she doing in this dark, hot place? Why did her body ache? Why were her legs numb?

Opening her eyes, several small shafts of light shining up through bullet holes in the ceiling brought the memory flooding back. The gravity of her situation cleared her mind.

She listened. Were they still there? Were they sleeping in her house? The idea made her suddenly indignant.

She was not sure if she was alone in the house, but she was sure of one thing. She had to go to the bathroom, and she was not going to do it in the attic.

Slowly, cautiously, she moved enough to slide the panel back. More light. No sounds. They must have gone. Moving shot needle-like pains through her numb legs, but she managed to reach the kitchen without attracting the attention of anyone. Looking up at the ceiling, she saw the string of bullet holes. How had they missed her? No wonder they didn't think there could be anyone alive up there. Christina was right. God's hand had to be protecting her.

Leaning against the wall for support, she saw herself mirroring her ex-husband's morning stance when he would wake in the kitchen, still in a stupor, and struggle to the bedroom. She couldn't help shaking her head at the incongruity.

Steadying herself, she made it to the bathroom.

Relief. She drew a deep breath of morning air. Today, she was alive. She could breathe.

Uweri noticed her arm was bleeding. She grabbed a wad of toilet paper and dabbed at the cut, carefully dropping the wad into the waste basket. She didn't want to mess up the house.

The idea struck her as humorous as she went into her once tidy living room. Furniture was smashed, lamps were on the floor, the front door was askew. The books remained on the shelf, untouched.

Not wanting to be seen, she backed up against the wall and cautiously peeked outside. They were still there at the bottom of the hill. Wisps of smoke came from what appeared to be vehicles lying in the ditch. She saw a bloody body lying in the yard across the street and wondered how many had been killed since she'd heard the first gun shot.

Feeling faint, she realized she had not eaten since lunch the day before. Keeping to the wall, she made her way back to the kitchen. The refrigerator was open and empty. Even the cupboards had been raided. Everything that could be eaten had been taken.

Hoping some fresh air would revive her, she made her way to the back door and opened it a crack. The smell of the garbage, intensified by the rising heat offended her, but it also offered the possibility of something to eat. She saw a couple of rotting bananas that someone had tossed out on a better day. A black dog looked at her and returned to foraging for his own breakfast. Hoping her neighbors couldn't see her, she scooted down low to pick up the bananas. They were too squishy to peel so she tore off one end and sucked out the contents.

Finishing one and starting on the other, she heard voices and her front door being scraped open.

Rowdy shouts followed. "Any Tutsi here? I haven't killed any for an hour. Come on, let's have some fun."

Only a strong survival instinct, generated by fear, could have overcome her repugnance at what she must do. That instinct propelled her into the trash heap. The dog jumped aside as she lunged under a pile of rotting banana leaves. Rats scurried as she burrowed her way deeper, trying not to disturb the surface of the garbage pile.

She heard the back door fly open, banging against the wall.

"Nothing out here except a scroungy dog."

"I wonder if it's a Tutsi."

A short staccato of gunfire, a brief whine, and she knew that she would no longer have to share her food store with anyone besides the rats.

The nightmare existence of the days that followed became a blur. Day and night Uweri rotated her hiding place from the oven-like crawlspace to the garbage heap, eating leaves and spoiled food, chasing away her little companions when they got too friendly. The smell of decaying garbage mingled with that of a decomposing carcass.

Eatable garbage grew scarce and hunger gnawed at her stomach. She would doze off and dream about the buffet at a local hotel where her husband had sometimes taken her, only to awaken to one of her little friends getting too familiar while looking for his own lunch.

There was plenty of time to think. Where had she gone wrong? Why did she ever leave her tribe? Did she just want to show them that she could really be somebody?

She tried to concentrate on the good times— her wedding, time spent with her friend, Kayitesi. Had she made it home safely? She thought of the birth of each of her children. Had she been a good mother? If she had only been a better wife, would she have her husband beside her today? To die alone with no one around but a dead dog was no way for one's life to end.

She would catch herself sobbing, disappointed in herself for having a "pity party." *No more of this!* she told herself and would again picture her two little girls. How precious they were and what joy they brought to her. Especially Christina. From a very early age, Christina had an unusual faith. When her father left the family, she seemed to easily trust God to be the one to hold her hand and take care of her. When there wasn't money for food or rent or new shoes for school, Christina would encourage Uweri. "Mommie, God has enough for us. He will take care of us, don't worry." Elizabeth adored her big sister and never let go of her when they went out of the house. Surely, no one would hurt the children. Umutomi would have taken them to church for sanctuary. She comforted herself with the knowledge that they would be safe there.

The days of heat and stench, of hunger and sleeplessness, of filth and fear, of background sounds of intermittent gunfire coming from the direction of the roadblock, had turned into weeks.

Uweri was careful to remain out of sight in her "upper room" sanctuary or in her facetiously named "mansion in the backyard." But, this day thirst and the thought of the kitchen faucet overcame her caution. She hadn't heard anyone in the house in the daytime for several days, so she felt safe. She was so hungry and thirsty and miserable she just wanted this to be over anyway.

Standing up by the back door, she knew she looked and smelled worse than the garbage heap. How she'd love to have a shower, but she didn't dare. She smiled at the thought of bumping into a Hutu in her present pungent state, visualizing him fleeing with nose clamped shut to escape this smelly creature.

Stepping into the kitchen, he was as surprised as she. He spun around, pointing his AK–47 at her, stuttering, "Who are you?"

"I live here."

"No, I mean are you a Hutu or a Tutsi?"

"I am neither." She reached down into her dress, praying the paper would still be there. The young man watched as she fumbled in her dress, letting the gun hang at his side, and stepped toward her.

She found the paper, pulled it out quickly, and held it out for him to see.

"See, I am neither."

He stopped and took the paper. "Are you Hutu or Tutsi?"

"Can't you see, I am neither." She moved and pointed to the top of the paper. "There, there is my tribe."

Realizing he probably couldn't read, she repeated the word "tribe, tribe."

He held up his gun, pointing it at her. "I need money. It's my turn to buy the drinks. Where is your money hidden?"

She remembered that she had folded her few bills and hidden them on her person, but she knew it would be dangerous to retrieve them while he looked on.

"Where is your money?" he shouted impatiently while striding toward her, bringing his gun to her face.

She crouched at his feet and looking up imploringly, said, "You have the power to kill me." She sensed a change of expression of his face. "And you have the power to let me live. I have no money to give you."

Head bowed, she began to pray, "God, don't let it hurt too much. I need to feel Your hand."

"I'll be back," shouted the young man angrily as he turned and went out the front door mumbling to himself, "I have to get money. It's my turn."

Watching through the window, she saw him go to the neighbor's house. He beat on the door with the butt of his rifle. She remembered the night that she had knocked and was told to leave.

The door opened. She recognized the wife's voice. "Wait, I'll get some..." Seconds later Uweri saw the neighbor hand out a wad of bills. The young man took them, stuck them in his pocket, backed off slightly, and raised his gun to her face. There was one quick blast. The soldier stepped back as she fell at his feet.

Uweri sunk to her knees, "Oh, God, what kind of people are we? Oh God, what have we become?"

There was no use hiding any more. They knew she was there. After their drinks they would be back. She sat on a chair in the middle of her living room...waiting. She was too weary to hide any longer. Momentarily forgetting about her children, death appeared a welcome relief.

They came within minutes. Five of them stood around her. They looked like children, except for the leader. He might have been all of twenty-one or twenty-two. The kids were obviously drunk, but he was not. One of the kids dropped his AK–47 on her lap. "Go ahead, shoot us," he taunted. She knew if she touched the gun it would give them all an excuse for killing her. "Go ahead, Tutsi, pick it up." Some one kicked her in the leg. "See, we are being fair. We are giving you a chance. Don't ever let anyone say the militia are cowards." She realized they still had a conscience.

The leader confronted her: "Who are you? Are you a Tutsi or a Hutu?"

She retrieved her document from inside her dress. "I am neither." Pulling out the paper, she unfolded it and handed it to him. "There! See, that is my tribe." This one could read and a look of surprise came across his face.

He stared at her. "This is my tribe.... I come from there as well." He handed the paper back to her. Turning to the other soldiers, he spoke firmly, "She is neither Tutsi or Hutu, she is of my tribe."

The young soldiers put down their guns. As Uweri stood, the gun on her lap fell to the floor. Someone picked it up.

The leader turned to the one who had killed her neighbor and commanded, "Put her in a vehicle and take her to where all the people are gathering. Go, she is neither Tutsi or Hutu. She is of my tribe."

As they left the house, she unconsciously muttered to herself, "His hand *is* on us. Yes, Christina, you were right. His hand is on us."

"What? What are you saying?"

"Nothing...nothing."

He led her outside and pointed her toward the roadblock as the others followed behind.

The Camps

I have become the ridicule of all my people—
Their taunting song all the day.
He has filled me with bitterness,
He has made me drink wormwood.
For the Lord will not cast off forever.
Though He causes grief, yet He will show compassion
According to the multitude of His mercies.
For He does not afflict willingly,
Nor grieve the children of men.
To crush under one's feet all the prisoners of the earth,
To turn aside the justice due a man before the face
of the Most High,
Or subvert a man in his cause—
The Lord does not approve
(Lamentations 3:14–15, 31–36).

How far away is hell? Those running for their lives thought they had found it.

The memory of watching their neighbors being massacred; of surviving by being buried under the bodies of their families, their friends, their neighbors, of taking off a piece of clothing, gently, almost ritualistically, placing it over the face of a loved one while whispering that there wasn't time for a decent burial; of dragging any survivors into the bushes. While escaping, hunger and exhaustion forced the exodus to stop for rest. Surely it would be safe for they must have finally left the militia behind.

But suddenly, the militia would step into the clearing, guns and grenades in hand. Worst of all were their taunts before they sprayed them with bullets.

Those left alive ran on. And now at last, the river.

Farmers who ordinarily would have been in their fields evaluating their crops, mothers who should have been in front of their little houses building fires to cook breakfast, children who normally would have been laughing and talking while putting on their best clothes to go to school, were instead coming out of the bushes carrying on their backs or heads everything they owned. As they stared at the river, they realized they would now lose everything. There was no question about what they must do. They set their meager belongings at their feet and stood at the river, the last obstacle before reaching some sort of safety. They didn't know what was on the other side, but they knew it couldn't be as bad as what they had just left.

Perhaps on the other side there would be a camp for refugees. After a respite they could regroup and try again to return to their own country and live in peace. It was the only hope they had left.

Silently, a woman with a child tied to her back slid into the water. The baby screamed as the cold washed over both of them. After a desperate swim that must have seemed an eternity long and an ocean wide, the mother crawled up the bank on the other side. Tripping, gasping for air, she started the long climb up the hill, following the crowd.

An elderly lady pleaded for someone to help her cross the river. A young man gave her a large banana leaf and held it under her chin, explaining how to use it as a float. She hesitated. Together they slid into the river. She began to sink. He held up her head as she put the leaf under her chin. He calmed her and she began to float. That fifty or sixty feet of water seemed like an uncrossable barrier. Relief flooded her face as she finally touched shore. Exhausted, but with the renewed strength of a survivor, she crawled up the embankment. The young man who loaned her the leaf was already halfway up the hill.

Some didn't make it. They just went under the water and down stream. The river accepted the load. During the previous couple of days thousands of bodies had floated by. Some still lay in the eddies, beginning to bloat.

A woman lost her grip on the hand of her child. The child sank. The woman dived once...twice...but the baby never reappeared and the woman began to wail. The child had been the last living member of her family. Now she was truly alone as she collapsed on the bank.

The procession of numbed survivors was oblivious to her state of grief. Though others could have reached out and touched her, they kept their eyes straight ahead, intent on their own climb up the embankment.

These scenarios were being repeated, with slight varia-tions, on borders all around Rwanda. From the north, south and east, hundreds of thousands of Rwandans swam rivers, crossed through jungles, ate anything that grew, in order to escape the militia.

Old men and women, most without shoes, all dirty and exhausted, trudged on. As long as they could move, there was still hope. Some carried rolled-up mats on their back. Others had used their mats to wrap the body of a loved one before leaving it at the side of the road for someone else to bury. Some had suitcases balanced on their heads. Others had bundles of firewood. They had been through civil war before and they knew they would need to cook their own food. One old man led a goat. Others carried live chickens or rabbits. An old woman struggled with a yellow plastic bucket containing a few articles of clothing. A younger woman carried a bundle of clothes on her head, pulling a young child along with one arm, while holding up an old lady with the other. A baby was tied to her back with a brightly colored piece of cloth.

Camps began to form. An exhausted Red Cross worker told anyone who would listen, "I was there when a million-and-a-half Kurds fled Northern Iraq, but they arrived over a three-week period. This is happening in only hours. What will we do?" Another shouted into a field phone, "We have no more than five tons of food. They are coming in at about ten thousand an hour. We need fifty thousand tons immediately or in a few hours we will have no food for them. Please help us, we can't let them starve."

The first to arrive fell to the ground, too exhausted to move. It would be the beginning of a refugee camp. As others came, they, too, would fall to the ground exhausted in body, overwhelmed in mind. Soon the children and young women would head for the trees. They had no machetes, the militia had seen to that, so they tore branches with their hands. Each party had to erect their own shelters. In a few hours all that was left of the trees were ugly stumps. Tomorrow, the next day, next week, they would need to walk for several hours to find any trees at all.

The little huts went up quickly as the branches were arranged. The next step was to join a line to receive a blue plastic cover for their new home, along with a day's ration of dried beans. Each group had to cook for themselves. Some carried cooking pots, but first there was the search for water. As evening came, a haze spread over the horizon blocking out the setting sun. Smoke from thousands of fires rose a few feet above the ground.

Tomorrow would be worse. In a normal camp of 200,000, 110 tons a day of human feces would be deposited on the ground. There were no sanitation facilities. That came later. As the clouds gathered in the evening and as the refugees huddled in their flimsy new homes, rain often washed off the blue plastic and joined the water running across the ground, spreading the feces so that the next day it would hardly be noticed. After the rain, some would go out with small cans to collect that same water. They had to have something to drink. They had to cook tomorrow's food. They passed the water around and each took a gulp of feces–laced, mud-colored gruel.

While this was taking place the "exiled" RPF army was moving down the center of Rwanda, driving the Hutu militia south. As the militia lost control, they hid their weapons and headed for the border camps, blending in with the refugees running from the assassinators. Most of the refugees were unaware of the disguised enemy in their midst or too frightened to voice objection.

Within days, the militia and others who had participated in the genocide joined forces and began to take control of the camps. They managed the food distribution centers.

The United Nations reported that the "regular refugees are now being held hostage by the militia." They had moved into the center of the camp so the true refugees, the women and children, would in effect become their human shields.

Their authority was temporarily interdicted by another enemy.

The first victim was no more than ten years old. She squatted on a rise of high ground, unable to stand. Another child held a tattered umbrella over her to protect her from the sun while dysentery drained her life away.

Tears ran down the father's face as he moved the umbrella aside to pick up the body of his daughter. Gently, he wrapped her in a piece of the blue plastic torn from the cover of their hut. Murmuring to her, he carried her to the edge of the camp and placed her on a stack of children— all dead. Cholera had arrived.

Cholera can be more deadly than AK–47s or machetes. Volunteer workers saw a child lying down and wondered if she was sleeping or dead. They knelt beside her and felt for a pulse. There was none so they picked her up and carried her to the pile of children's bodies. Just then, she moved her head. "She's not dead. We can't just leave her with the dead." So they gently lowered her to the ground and moved on to the next victim. Volunteers had to struggle to insert needles into the arms of the dying, but precious liquid just might save a life. This girl's waterless eyes looked up at the volunteer who was probing to find a vein for the needle. The girl finally asked to be left alone. "Don't hurt me any more." The volunteer moved on with the needle and bag of fluid to another who might survive.

A young UN worker, near collapse, was unable to bear any more. He choked out his feelings, "This is closer to hell than I ever wanted to get."

But this wasn't hell. There are no ministering angels in hell; the camps had many. They served wherever they could be used, without sleep, without rest—volunteers from colleges, from missions organization, from Europe and North America. They arrived with trucks of water to replace the cupfuls of disease-laden sewage. There were enough needles and enough water to halt the disease. The angels with their supplies won the battle. We don't know many of their names, but God knows. They received their reward when the children gazed into their eyes.

With the cholera under control, the secret militia in the inner camp resumed their covert rule. The exiled RPF was slowing taking control of the homeland. They pleaded for all refugees to return to their towns and villages. They promised there would be no persecution, only justice. Many wanted to return but the guilty Hutus wanted the protection that came from the cordon of refugees around them. As relief workers struggled under tremendous odds to get food to the camps, the Hutu militia, now equipped with radios and cars, kept track of where the next food distribution would occur and raced to get there first. Many of them, drunk or stoned on marijuana, stopped convoys and demanded bribes or a portion of the supplies for them to sell.

Frustrated, but without the means to prevent the thefts and violence, the United Nations commander reported that "many refugees in the camps are effectively being held hostage. When buses come to take people back to Rwanda, they are surrounded by the militia who run their finger across their necks, a sign that refugees who leave will risk having their throats cut, not by the RPF, but by the Hutus."

At night, these same young men jog around the camps shouting, "We want blood; we want revenge." They say they are loyal Rwandans training to return to free their country, but the UN reports that "the jogging is to make the refugees think a war is still going on, to scare them away from the idea of going back."

In the camps the militia watches and listens. They give warnings that all are under surveillance and if anyone tries to leave, they will not make it to the bus. The women and children are watched when they leave their huts. If the men get up to join them, they are confronted. Some are taken back into their huts—dead.

Take the horror of the massacres, the harrowing escape, the long dark nights in the camp, the standing in the hot sun for food, the fear of the Hutus, the death of the children and multiply it by 1.2 million in Zaire, 200,000 in Burundi, 700,000 in Tanzania, 300,000 in camps in Rwanda—a total of 3 million—and you begin to comprehend the measure of human suffering that is seen in the dry eyes that have cried so much there are no tears left. Stand on the river bank and weep with Jeremiah who cried out: "My eyes will weep bitterly and run down with tears, because the LORD's flock has been taken captive" (Jeremiah 13:17).

As Uweri followed the soldier down the slope to the roadblock, she struggled to keep from breaking down. She couldn't believe what she saw: dismembered bodies on the street, trucks filled with bodies passing the checkpoint, burned-out cars, no one around except the militia—and more bodies. How many did they kill? She was flooded with fresh fear—and thankfulness. She saw some children's bodies. Where were her girls? At the church? Buildings had been burned. Would churches have been burned?

Her young escort sensed her horror at what she saw. "Bad, isn't it? Well, they asked for it. They killed our president and now they want to make us slaves again. Them and their stupid cows. Never again. We are in control now." The words seemed to be spoken more to assure himself than to convince her.

"I'm glad I didn't have to kill you. I have killed too many already. I wish I could stop. We were told if there was no Tutsi blood on our machetes they would be covered with our blood. Those were our orders. I wish it would all end. I see you don't believe me."

"I don't understand. I just don't understand. Why all this killing?"

"We hear the exiled RPF is moving south. If they are, we are going to be in trouble. Well, I talked too much."

He drove on, silently, until they came to a main road crowded with a massive procession of people shuffling along like a defeated army.

The driver slammed on the breaks. She fell forward and grabbed the dash.

"This is as far as I go. You can join the crowd." He motioned for her to get out.

She didn't need any encouragement.

He honked his horn, called out some obscenities to those in his way, made a U-turn, and with tires squealing headed back to his roadblock.

In shock, Uweri moved with the crowd. *This many people,* she thought, *must know where they are going.* No one spoke. Most were women, some old men. Some carried belongings on their heads. Others had babies tied on their backs. They were like a defeated army, shuffling its way to prison barracks.

Some had wounds wrapped in rags. Some were being supported by others. Some just fell by the side of the road, too tired or too sick to go farther. They lay down beside the dead, expecting to join them.

A Hutu, with an armed soldier on each side, was selling food. Uweri hadn't eaten in days. She reached for her money and then decided against it. She would need the money later. She watched as a woman got a couple of bananas and handed a bill to the young man. He stuck it in his pocket. She held her hand out for change. The other two pushed her away, cussing her. They were giving no change.

Uweri's feet were burning, and she suddenly realized she had no shoes on. But what could she do. And where was she going?

All these people must be going somewhere where there was safety. She asked several. Some simply stared at her but one replied, "Anywhere where they won't kill me."

Another looked at her as if she were stupid, "To Zaire, of course."

Zaire? she thought. *That's miles from here. It will take days, weeks. I can't walk that far. Besides, when we get there they probably won't let us cross the border.* Her silent conversation with herself came to an abrupt halt. She heard a familiar voice. Could it be? She was afraid to turn around for fear it was her imagination. Then she heard it clearly.

"Mommie! Mommie!"

Uweri turned and dropped to her knees, holding out her arms as Christina ran to her. They fell back to the ground, hugging and weeping as they embraced.

"Mommie, I knew I'd find you. I knew God would take care of us."

"Christina, where are Elizabeth and Umutomi?"

Christina was immediately subdued, "I lost her. Yesterday. I don't know where she is. Umutomi took us to a church. She's gone, too."

"But the church was a safe place, wasn't it? That's where we went last time to be safe."

"No, Mommie. They broke down the doors and threw in tear gas...and then," she paused, "and then they began to shoot and kill everyone. We ran for the doors. Some people fell down and couldn't get up. Some got out. Elizabeth and I got separated. I ran as hard as I could until I fell down. I couldn't get up for a long time. I crawled into a burned out house and fell asleep. When I woke up I saw these people walking and I just walked with them.

"But don't worry, Mommie. God is taking care of baby

sister, somewhere. Wait and see. We are in God's hands and so is Elizabeth...don't cry, Mommie. Mommie? Are you all right?"

Unable to speak at first, she finally sobbed, "I don't deserve you."

After more embraces, they both stood. An Old Lady, with a thin cigar in her mouth, listened and watched them from a wizened face. Avoiding eye contact, she turned and walked on.

Uweri and Christina, hand in hand, rejoined the walking crowd.

"We are going to Zaire, Mommie."

"But dear, we could never make it that far."

"But we will, Mommie, we will. God will take us there."

Uweri wiped her eyes. Tears of anxiety over Elizabeth and gratitude for Christina's safety mingled with tears of shame for her lack of faith.

The crowd grew as they shuffled along together. There was less and less talk.

After a day of walking Uweri left a bloody footprint with each step. Oh, to rest her feet in cool water.

A shout from her daughter brought her back to reality.

"Where are you going? Come back," called Uweri, too weak to chase her. Christina raced through the crowd. Hesitating up ahead, searching the crowd, Christina saw again what she had dared to hope she would see. Big sister caught the hand of a lonely little girl and the two girls raced back to meet their Mommie—just the way they used to run to meet the bus each day.

Uweri, overcome with gratitude, could only laugh and

cry. Their family was back together again.

The Old Lady had watched the drama from a distance, but listened closely as Christina reminded her mother again and again, "God *was* holding our hand! He brought us back together. I knew He would! I knew He would!"

The road narrowed as they left the city. Shady bushes alongside the road were inviting. Uweri thought it would be easy to sit down and rest, but would she be able to get up again?

Then something happened that made the blood left on the road from her feet seem terribly insignificant. Before anyone could run, a jeep loaded with militia came down the side of the road and braked abruptly several hundred yards from Uweri and the girls. As the dust settled some of the people began to run. There was the sound of machine guns and the warning, "Don't run. We'll get all of you."

The three of them stood frozen, holding onto each other. *Oh, God, don't let it end like this.*

The militia confronted three young men and two women. There was some shouting, and then one of them stood back, raised his AK–47 and fired. Before Uweri could turn her daughters' heads, the bodies fell to the ground. No one breathed. The militia moved a few feet closer. They took two other young men and one older woman; holding their guns to their heads, they marched them off the road. In a few moments the sounds Uweri dreaded cut through the air once more. The soldiers came swaggering back to the road, jumped in their jeep, and came straight toward Uweri. She and several others jumped to the side of the road as they passed.

When the dust settled, the people began to move on as though nothing had happened.

"That's what they did at the church. They are very bad men."

Uweri reached down and ran her fingers through Elizabeth's hair. "Yes, dear, they are very bad men." The three rejoined the exodus. Only now, Uweri did not even look down at the blood-stained footprints.

Moments later, people in front of them began to shout and run into the bushes. All Uweri could think of was that the militia was coming back to kill more Tutsis. Christina followed them, calling back to Uweri and Elizabeth, "Mommie, it's not soldiers, someone has found bananas." A young girl appeared from the bushes carrying a large bunch of bananas on her shoulder. She tossed them to the ground, indicating they belong to everyone. Christina tore off several and ran to share them with Uweri and her little sister.

As the miles passed, some of the stronger people would move out from the road, looking for anything that was edible. They brought back bananas most of the time, but sometimes a deserted farm would yield some greens. No one tried to sell the food. They probably would not have lived very long.

After walking for a couple of hours in the morning, Uweri and the children would rest in the shade of a bush. One day they passed an old women's body that had a plastic cup tied to her skirt. Since she wouldn't need it any longer, Uweri took it. Each time they rested Christina looked for water. Sometimes she found it and sometimes she didn't. Uweri lived in constant fear of dehydration. She often saw people lying by the road who had no cup; if there was a stream nearby, Christina would spend several hours bringing water, one cup at a time, to those unable to get their own.

In the late afternoon, Uweri had to force herself to stand up. The pain was nearly unbearable, but she had to go on. As she walked, the girls walked beside her so she could lean on their shoulders.

Almost everyone seemed absorbed in their own pain. However, they were often conscious of the Old Lady's presence near them. Several times Uweri saw her and the girls smile at each other.

All day long motley vehicles pushed their way through the walking masses with horns honking and their young men shouting warnings that there would be no free rides. From time to time, the vehicles would be abandoned at the side of the road, out of fuel, with flat tires or a burned-out motor. When the vehicle died, the driver ran for his life into the bushes. There would be no refunds.

The dread of the daily encounters with the militia, the search for food and the onward march continued day after day. It would take at least three weeks to reach Zaire.

One morning they came to a fork in the road. "Girls, look," she pointed to a sign with an arrow. "I have a cousin who lives in that village." She knew that it was in the same direction as the border. Eventually, both roads led to Zaire.

Christina was excited, "Maybe she'll give us some food and we can rest at her house."

"But it will take a couple of days to get there. Do you think we can make it?"

"Come on, Mommie, we can make it. God will help us

get there."

Elizabeth said, "Maybe we can just stay there."

Uweri tried to remember what she could about her cousin. She hadn't seen her in years. For a moment she hesitated as she remembered her cousin had married a Hutu. Well, at least he would still be alive. "Let's go find my cousin."

As they rounded a corner, they saw an old pickup truck. It was loaded with people standing up. The driver was standing behind it, calling out that he could give them a ride. He had room for a couple more.

Uweri asked where he was going. He was going by the village where her cousin lived.

"How much for me and my two girls?

The amount was more than she had. She looked at him with pleading eyes as he turned to others, selling space in the already-crowded pickup.

The Old Lady approached the driver, spoke to him quietly, gave him some money and went to the back of the pickup. Several hands lifted her on, impatiently waiting to get a full load so they could be on their way.

Uweri stooped and retrieved her money. Holding it out to the driver, she made another attempt, "Look, this is all I have." She pointed to her bleeding feet. "I can't walk much farther. The girls take up only a tiny space. They can almost stand between my legs."

He reached out for her money and said, "Go, get up."

Hands reached down and pulled up the three sets of arms.

The breeze felt good as the truck moved slowly along.

The driver honked at those walking in the road, trying to clear a path to drive through.

Uweri was troubled as she realized she hardly noticed anymore the dead bodies by the side of the road.

The girls chatted to each other about what their cousin might feed them.

Uweri discovered that standing amidst this shoving, cursing group was almost as painful as walking. The sun was directly overhead. Several collapsed. There was no room for them to fall down. They stood, held erect by those leaning against them. The miles and hours passed slowly.

At last the truck stopped. The driver got out.

"This is it, this is as far as we go. The border is that way." Uweri asked where the village was. The driver pointed to a side road, "Just down there."

The girls led the way. Excited, they encouraged Uweri to hurry. They were hungry.

"There it is!" they shouted. "Where does she live?"

Uweri didn't know the exact place, but it shouldn't be hard to find. Everyone would know everyone.

They passed an empty house and saw a small store. An old man was selling meager supplies of food. The children looked at it longingly, but knew they had no money.

Uweri asked if he knew her cousin and gave her name. He pointed to a house down the road. As they picked up speed, approaching the house, they could almost taste the food, feel the rest. Uweri would soak her feet in cool water.

They came to the house and knocked. No one answered. They knocked again.

The door was opened slightly. Uweri smiled, calling out her cousin's name. "It's me, your cousin Uweri."

The door was quickly closed. "Go away. You will get us all killed, go away."

The girls looked at their mother, shocked. "She's your cousin. She can't do that," cried Christina.

"Please," Uweri pleaded through the closed door, "at least give us something to eat. We are so hungry."

Christina chimed in, "Give us some food and we will leave."

Thinking there would be no response, they turned to leave. Just then, the door opened slightly and a banana leaf, piled high with rice, was shoved onto the door stoop.

Uweri picked it up and the three of them quickly consumed it all.

Somewhat refreshed, they headed back to the main road.

Approaching the main road, they saw crowds of people sitting. The militia had stopped them from going further. Too many were leaving, they said. They were trying to persuade the people to go back home, but they all sat down instead, refusing to move.

Uweri found slight relief in sitting. Elizabeth pointed across the road, "Look, there is Auntie. She must have waited for us."

Uweri saw the Old Lady. She was leaning against a tree, not making eye contact with anyone.

Forgetting about her, Uweri and the girls tried to get in a comfortable position so they could get some sleep.

In the middle of the night word came down the line. They could move forward.

Uweri wakened the girls. Elizabeth didn't move, so Uweri picked her up and placed her head on her shoulder. With Christina hanging on to her arm, they joined the shuffling procession.

"Look, Mommie, there's a truck like ours, and it's waiting for people to get on."

It was yesterday's scene repeated. Only this time the truck was only partly filled. She soon found out why. The price had gone up considerably.

It was still at least 30 kilometers to the border. Uweri knew she could not walk that far. Her feet were raw. She would have to stay behind.

"No, Mommie, come on," Christina begged.

"I can't walk any further, I just can't. Look at my feet."

"No, Mommie, let's go ask that man. Maybe he will let us back on the truck."

She knew it was impossible. They had no money.

"Come on," Christina insisted, tugging her mother.

They walked up to the driver.

"I have no money. I can't walk. Please have mercy."

He repeated the price, staring past her into the distance.

The Old Lady approached the driver, wearing her dour face. She reached into her dress and pulled out a gold medallion and showed it to the driver. For the first time, they heard her speak. "This is worth much more. Here, take it."

The driver greedily grabbed it before she changed her mind. The Old Lady got on the pickup and the driver motioned to Uweri and the children to get on, too.

"Come on, we have enough. Let's go."

This time the truck was not so crowded.

The Old Lady spoke, still staring ahead. "I've been watching you and your children. Without them you would be dead beside the road. I have seen the peace of God on the face of your children, not on your face, but on theirs. I have heard them say their God has them in His hand. He surely must. They have a very powerful God. I am not of your faith, but I wish my God was that powerful. May He bless me for helping them."

Christina looked up at her mother and smiled, as if to say "See, I told you so."

They had been riding less than an hour when the pick-up stopped.

The driver got out, "Militia ahead. They are checking ID cards. Better get it ready for them."

The slow, but unfaltering progress of the militia was accompanied by the sounds of certain death.

Uweri was sure this was the end. She tried to show a brave face to her girls, but she silently prayed, "God, have you brought us this far only to let them kill us? I'll stay," she bargained, "but let the girls get to safety. Don't let them be killed."

"Let me see your ID."

"This is all I have. You see it identifies my tribe."

"This is worthless. You are a Tutsi, aren't you?"

"No, can't you see I am neither Tutsi nor Hutu."

"If I don't kill you now, Tutsi, someone else will kill you later."

The Old Lady walked up the soldier and said, "I see by your hat that you are a Muslim." He nodded. "This is my daughter-in-law and grandchildren. If you kill them Allah will be very, very angry. He will torture you with more than that machete you carry so bravely. You will never have peace. You will spend forever running from the terrible things you are doing."

The soldier pointed to the side of the road, "The grandchildren go on. The mother stays."

Christina hung on to Uweri's hand. "No, Mommie, if they kill you they will have to kill us, too. Let's die together. We are not afraid." Christina tugged on Uweri's hand, leading her to the side of the road.

The soldier, as though he didn't see or hear them, walked on to the next group of people.

A few moments later, Uweri and the children crawled back on the truck and began the final leg of their journey to the border.

Children: The Innocent Victims

"Let the little children come to Me, and do not forbid them;
for of such is the Kingdom of God."
And He took them up in His arms, laid His hands on them,
and blessed them
(Mark 10:14,16).

If you were back home, you might hear sirens indicating the arrival of paramedics to attend to someone in physical distress. A jackhammer might be heard tearing up the street to replace the broken sewer line, causing the neighbors to hold their noses and complain about the noise. You might be meeting a friend for coffee and decide to stay for lunch, since you can easily call home and leave a message.

None of those things happen here. There are only the sick, the dying, the victims, and the almost overpowering smell of human waste. There are no streets, no coffee shops...and no 9-1-1.

This is a refugee camp, or as one jeans-clad photojournalist titled it, "a descent into hell."

To understand the depth of the descent, take a slow walk with me through the camp.

Upon entering, the children tug at your legs. You try to outpace them but the little ones keep up, their smiling, hopeful faces looking up to you. They try to reach into your pocket, but not for money. What they want can't be bought. You pull your hand out of your pocket and suddenly each finger is grabbed by a sweaty little hand. You can't rub your neck forever, so the second hand comes down. The same thing happens. Ten fingers, ten little children. No one looks to the left or to the right, only straight up into your face. More of them walk in front of you, holding on to your leg. Those who have hold of the fingers are now in control. With their free hands they push the others away. They continue to follow at a distance—part of a parade of shame.

One of the little boys holding on to a finger has an inflamed gash across his shoulders and neck. The mark of the machete.

The big eyes beg answers to questions that have no answers. *Can you find my mother, my father, my brother, my sister? Can you make it all right? Can you give me food? I'm hungry. Can you let the rest go and tightly hold me in your arms?*

Slowly you make your way past the little make-shift huts. Women, probably widows, sit in front stoking what is left of a dying fire, attempting to cook today's food that someone else stood in line for ten hours to get. The children don't see what you see. They see only you.

It is easy to understand why Jesus loved to be close to the children and why He admonished us to take care of them. You see in their miniature faces not just their cries for help, but their innocence, not yet totally destroyed by adult hate.

You pass several shelters and stop. One child, no bigger than the smallest one holding onto your fingers, lies unmoving. A young girl squats beside him, massaging his leg. Is he dead? People won't know until the body starts to swell in the tropical sun. Then they often will throw him away like a broken toy.

A young girl, just a child herself, looks up from her cooking pot, while holding on her lap a child, maybe two years old—the age when most children start talking, but not this one. He is too traumatized. He buries his head against her and she sheepishly, through an interpreter, explains, "He has no mother or father. They were killed. I found him out there." She points her chin out to indicate somewhere in the distance. "I had to pick him up, someone had to." She hugs him and you and your band of children move on.

Another stop. The camp dispensary overflows. This is not the kids' favorite place. They know that those who come here usually don't leave, at least not alive. They tug at your fingers.

Lying by himself, a boy listlessly, through swollen eyes, looks up at you and your little entourage. One of the ten says, "He's dying. Cholera," and then tugs on your finger to move on as if, "It's really not important, let's go." Another tragedy of everyday life in a refugee camp.

A very young, but exhausted, nurse volunteers information about the children. "Many of them are totally traumatized, too frightened to speak." She places a plastic cup to a small child's lips. "They are too frightened to ask for water, so we have to keep offering it to them or they will dehydrate. They can die in a couple of hours. This little one has a high fever, but she may get well. Her wounds will heal, but I'm not sure her soul ever will."

Some still carry machete marks, but all bear the marks of the cruelty of the big people that they trusted. But will they ever trust us again? "The only one here who will probably not remember this place is this one." She pointed to what appeared to be a rag. As she unwrapped the bundle to reveal a wizened face, she went on, "She's just a few weeks old. She was found still clinging to the breast of her murdered mother."

For several hours the walk continues, until you are at the perimeter of the camp. Over there is where you came in. The kids sense it. Some try to grasp your finger with both hands, not wanting to let go. You are their only hope. They tighten their grip as if to say, *But you are a grownup, you can help us. Find our mothers, our fathers. You can give us food. You can give us medicine to heal us. You can take us home. You can wake us up from this nightmare.* You slowly raise your arms and one by one the children let go and, for the first time, their eyes go from your face to the ground. There's one last pleading glance at you and then, hope lost again, they walk away.

The children have been loosed from your fingers, but not from your heart. As you walk toward your Land Rover, you long to turn and run after them, gather each one up in your arms and take them with you. But you know it is impossible. There are thousands of them needing an anchor. Your hands feel disconnected, at loose ends. You are told there are more children, maybe a hundred thousand, still roving the countryside in small bands, taking care of each other.

Now it's your turn to look up with pleading eyes. "Oh, God, take them in Your arms and have mercy on the children."

"There is hope in your future, says the LORD, that your children shall come back to their own border" (Jeremiah 31:17).

Uweri noticed that the militia seemed to be disappearing. Maybe the rumors were true that the RPF had come out of exile and were retaking the country.

The driver of the pickup was finding it more and more difficult to pass through the masses of people on the road who were oblivious to his honking or cursing. Finally, he just gave up, got out, and disappeared. Realizing their ride had ended, Uweri and the children, along with the others, crawled down and joined the shuffling masses drawing nearing the border. The Old Lady melted into the milling crowd.

As they made their way along the road they saw families tending to their sick and bodies wrapped in grass mats, waiting to be buried. For those, it was the end of their journey.

The pace slowed even more as Europeans with Red Cross armbands shouted, "Form four lines! Form four lines!" Uweri and the children joined a line and again they waited. The heat, the pain of standing, the odors, were almost more than Uweri could take.

Slowly, one family at a time, the line moved forward. As the sun descended they moved, trying to catch the slight breeze that began to blow.

Finally, Uweri told the girls, "I can see the checkpoint. We're getting close." She reached down into her dress to make sure she had her paper. Another hour passed. It was getting dark. There were only a few people ahead of them. The girls were excited that the trip would soon be over. They would be in a refugee camp at last.

Their chatter was interrupted by an animal-like groan from their mother. They both grabbed her arm, "Mommie, Mommie, what's wrong?

Uweri stifled her moans with her hand as she gaped at the official at the head of the line.

She closed her eyes. "It's all right, Mommie. It's all right" comforted the girls, not understanding their mother's distress.

She looked up again. There was no doubt about it. It was him. She had not seen him in two years. They had worked closely together at the trucking company in Kigali. There were even times when their glances, their laughter, their conversation indicated they might be more than fellow employees.

Then one day the friendship came to an abrupt end. One of the executives was promoted and his job became available. Her friend wanted the job and was boasting to her that it was his. He was the kind of person that could be Hutu one day and a Tutsi the next, if it advanced his career. His ambition to be important far exceeded his abilities.

She remembered every detail of the day she walked out of the company president's office with the job. He walked by her, glaring with such hatred, it frightened her. He slammed the door and never came back to work. She had not seen him since then, until now.

There he was, checking the IDs. At his command were the officials who could step aside and allow the refugee to pass into Zaire, or could refuse entrance and firmly point the way back.

Uweri was now next in line.

Looking at the ground, she moved to the table and laid down her identification paper. Without looking up, he took it and began to read it. His arm jerked as he stared at it. She could hear him mutter, "Uweri?" He looked up and their eyes met. He stood, a broad smile spread across his face. He reached his arms across the table, put them around her, and said, "Uweri, my cousin, how wonderful to see you and your little girls." Then, whispering in her ear, "I thought you must be dead."

Without looking down, he wrote something on the paper, turned to a uniformed assistant, and barked the command, "Escort my cousin and her children to the border."

"Mommie, he's not our cousin."

"Shhh."

The human barrier parted, a young man stepped forward and took her ID paper, indicating they were to follow him. She looked back. Their eyes met and he turned away, calling out, "Next."

Tears flowed as Christina called, "Come on, Mommie, come on."

The two little girls flanked the young officer, one on each side. They looked up at him and smiled as they each took one finger of his hand, and walked toward the camp. He smiled back.

Uweri looked upward...and wept. She knew that she, too, held Someone's hand.

An MK's Journal

Ah, Lord GOD!
Behold, I cannot speak,
for I am a youth
(Jeremiah 1:6).

*H*aving lived through one war, one police action, and one Asian quagmire, having viewed films of Auschwitz and watched bodies float down the Pearl River during the Cultural Revolution, having waited beside a chopper on a tarmac in Vietnam while body bags carrying U.S. Marines were being unloaded, and having stood on the border of Cambodia as thousands fell across, many dead before anyone could help them up, I find myself becoming desensitized to human suffering.

Perhaps I'm becoming callous. I'm no longer seeing bodies float by, but numbers. I'm not participating in a mother's grief as she holds a dead child in her arms, but loathing those responsible for these tragedies.

The camps and the children may be described with more sensibility by an eighteen-year-old MK (missionary kid) high

*school senior, Jon Sommers. This chapter is taken from the
pages of Jon's journal.*

A blast of hot, dirty air swept through the cargo bay of
the C–130 cargo plane as the rear door swung down and
open. Very humid. My first impression of this hell was the
sight of a couple of dozen kids running behind our plane
as we taxied into our allotted spot. Like some kind of sur-
real game, they ran behind with smiles on their faces,
laughing as the backdraft of our four giant engines would
knock one of them over. If I could have seen, just before
we landed, the mass of people on the runway scattering
out of the way of our flight, I would not have thought so
much of their game, but as for now the contrast of torn
and ragged clothes and smiles amidst hunger and pain was
enough to touch my heart. Little did I know how much
more my heart would be touched during my stay in Goma
and Bukavu. I will never be the same.

Directly outside the airport in Goma were mass graves.
On these graves were simple, rough crosses, each one rep-
resenting two thousand people buried beneath it. I count-
ed at least seven of them. (It was said there were ten.)
Between fourteen and twenty thousand people needlessly
dead, buried under the very symbol of life—the cross. I
couldn't help but wonder how many of those had bowed
their knee to their grave marker and its Master.

The town of Goma itself was an unimpressive, typical
African semi-small town. The sight that struck me as
being the first of many atypical impressions was the
incredible mass of humanity everywhere my eye could see.
Growing up in East Africa, I was accustomed to the
throngs ever-present along the roadside in the cities and
towns, but the sheer masses along the streets of Goma

shocked me. I did not realize this was just a glimpse of the 1.4 million camped in the surrounding area around Goma. Not even in Nairobi had I seen so many people packed onto one place.

There were three main camps of refugees around Goma. Two to the north, Kimbumba and Katale, each with around 400,000 or more refugees in them. One to the west with the same amount. I visited each of them—an experience I will never be able to forget or remember without feeling. Coming around a corner, in a car, a trickle of people on the road, I was suddenly confronted with people as far as I could see.

Small shacks, about the size of a Boy Scout tent, made out of sticks and grass, maybe covered with a UNHCR tarp, dotted the ravaged, hazy landscape for a distance of about two miles. Entire families with children and babies lived in these tiny, rain-soaked, lice-filled, disease-infested shacks, surviving on a small daily ration provided by the UN. On one side of the road was the camp, on the other side, nature's urinal: a nasty, feces-filled landscape dotted with squatting kids, dying from cholera or dysentery. Scattered here and there were those who were already dead—kids who fell over dead while squatting. It's always the children that suffer the most. Later on I asked a man if he was hungry, and he said no, but that his kids were starving to death. He was fat and his kids were dead. The innocent always suffer.

Wrapped in a kanga, covered with flies, and stiff from rigor mortis, a dead child lay by a water tank at a small clinic a little ways from the camp. No one mourned for him. No one took the time to bury him in the sharp, unforgiving lava rock and dust that made up the soil. No one had the energy. No one gave a damn. Death was everywhere. What else is new?

At the house in Bukavu, the Parkers ran a feeding program that began with around a hundred women with kids, then, by the time we left, was up to around a thousand. Every day before the feeding, a Rwandan pastor would preach in their language—this was the real food that kept them going. One day, during the singing that always preceded the preaching, something broke. The Spirit moved on the hearts and bodies of the people and spontaneously many of them began to dance. It was so precious to see people who had nothing, many who were widows who saw their husbands slaughtered before their eyes, put aside the past and dance with simple joy before the Lord. That was a breakthrough, for every day since, there have been women and children who stand and dance before the Lord. Cultural or not, this dancing—to see people free to express any joy in this situation—was intense.

A malnourished girl, rib cage protruding, eyes sunken, but a fierce determination on her face, walks with an empty plastic cup across the driveway, each step an effort. She stumbles once or twice, but keeps going, her battered, emaciated body trembling with the effort. She reaches the corner of the drive where the cups are placed for washing. The lady working there at the dishwashing station reaches for her cup, but the girl refuses to give it to her, instead finding the exact place in the tray where she thinks it should go. She sets it down, her task finished. She just wanted to put the cup away by herself—a mix of gratitude and determination. Those of us standing there witnessing the scene all had to brush tears from our eyes. Later, we would see this same girl dance and sing before the Lord as her strength returned. Memories like this don't fade away.

To see the eyes is to see the soul. To touch the soul is to touch the person. I have never seen so many dead people as I saw in Goma and Bukavu. Alive in body, but living for nothing. Mindless shells, hopeless souls. To see is to touch, to feel, to share. The gaze of the soul. I touched many dead people. I felt the pain, the sorrow, the helplessness and bitterness that screamed from within through hollow, dead, unfeeling eyes...

I pray that my soul gave something they needed—that the Spirit used that contact to impart some life, some hope. If I touched their inner death, could they have somehow touched my inner life? The "faceless masses" are not so faceless in my memories. To make eye contact is to touch a soul. A soul touched is not faceless. My dreams are haunted by the faces, the eyes, the sorrow, the hopelessness. I sleep, but I don't rest. Is there a way to touch others in an instant, a gaze given as your car passes them on the street? A way to touch their soul and impart the life of God—a touch of love? Where language and race divides, the human soul is unified. Could it be that I have touched people in the same way they have touched me? That instead of their sleep being plagued by memories of dead eyes, that they would remember a young muzungu who passed by them in a car and whose eyes gave them hope? Could it be?

Dear God, let it be. I cannot carry the memories without knowing that somehow I made a difference in someone's life. Even one. Even one would be worth it. For even one you died. I wonder how many people you touched with just a glance, a simple touch of souls? I wonder how many remembered the life and love they saw in your eyes while on the cross and turned to you years later in a sweat-soaked bed, their sleep plagued by dreams of the Man they crucified? Dear God, let it be...

It has been said that in the Bukavu area, because of the French safety zone, the refugee men from the ages of fifteen to twenty-five have killed about forty people each. While reaching out to these people, the thoughts, the sneaky little demons, enter your mind: *This man has probably hacked a whole family to death. I wonder what he would do to you if he had the chance? I wonder if he would do it again? He's looking at you. Look at his eyes, he hates you. He wants to kill you.* Those thoughts are perfectly human and normal.

It's hard to remember we serve a God who has the beautiful attribute of forgetfulness. He is capable—and would love doing it—of saying to a Hutu murderer who has been redeemed by His Son, "What murders? I don't remember any murders. Gabriel, do you remember any murders this man committed?" Gabriel, of course, would look in that vast and wonderfully forgetful book and reply no. If the God we serve chooses to forget all the wrongs done to Him (for each wrong done is really directed to Him), then we must learn to put aside our humanity and look beyond sin to the soul. It is absolutely necessary if we are to survive and excel in a sin-filled world. We must look at every person as God would see him. We must remember to forget. Somebody called this philosophy "flippant, given the gravity of the situation." I would much rather think of it as biblical—not easy, but a command to be followed. It is easy to remember, for we are human and never forget. It is hard, and a test of godly character, to forget....

Someone asked me about the spiritual dynamics of this

whole situation, the sense I got from the area and people. Well, if you can imagine a room with petrol spread on the floor at about a half-inch level and you walking in with flint on the soles of your shoes, scuffing your feet, that's some of what it's like. Very tense. As if a single spark could ignite the entire populace of refugees into murderous action in an instant. Like a spiritual time-bomb, the area is fused with short-tempered souls and frustrated young men spurred on by demonic-inspired thoughts and memories of past sins. The blood of the past is never enough. Sin and death breed more sin and death until the cycle is broken....

The drives through the camps are what stick in my mind. The mass of mindless, hopeless, loveless, possessionless, Godless people, wandering aimlessly to find their small ration of food or water, just holding on to life. For what? What hope is there for these people? If they stay, then hundreds of thousands more will die. If they go, they face the fear of the unknown. The relatives of those they slaughtered wait for them in their homeland. So once again the innocent suffer. The children die for the sins of the fathers. The strong, the weak, the small, the innocent, the children, die without hope. *Dear God, may I never complain about anything again. You've given me so much. When I see the helplessness of others, my arrogance and selfishness becomes a stench in my nostrils, as it has always been in yours....*

Well, it is later. About four months later. The memories are still there, as well as the pain for the people in such a plight. It's not an experience to forget. My daily prayer is to be like Christ. There's nothing I can do to help anyone in any situation without Him. *Dear God,* keep me broken before you. May I never become cold or callous to the needs of others. May I see with your eyes and hear with your ears and feel with your heart. Amen.

Part II
...Into the Light

*If we walk in the light
as He is in the light,
we have fellowship with one another,
and the blood of Jesus Christ His Son cleanses us from all sin*
(1 John 1:7).

Introduction
to Part II

The veteran newsman, callused by the cynicism of his profession and impressed with his power as an opinion maker, cleared his throat, stared into the camera and concluded his report: "There are some stories that can never be told. This [Rwanda] is one of them. No pictures, or words can convey the enormity of the suffering. It is a calamity of epic proportions, so massive in size and scope that the truth of it is far beyond journalism's reach."

It is neither a judgment nor a criticism to point out that, as is often the case, the mass media is both right and wrong. Wrong, in saying Rwanda's story "can never be told." It can. And right, in that it is, indeed, "beyond journalism's reach."

U.S. Department of Justice attorney Gary Haugen, reporting in *Christianity Today*, tells the story very graphically when he writes of "tendon by tendon butchery. The eviscerating of pregnant women, the casting of screaming babies into mass graves to be buried alive, the one-by-one hacking to death of thousands of defenseless people."

MK, Jon Sommers, went beyond the reaches of journalism as he wrote in his personal diary, "I have seen many dead people. Alive in body, but living for nothing. I feel the pain, the sorrow, the hellishness, the bitterness that screams from within through hollow, dead, uncaring eyes."

To tell the story, and to go beyond the reaches of journalism, one must reach beyond history, politics, and ethnicity.

The defining moment for me came on a grassy plain outside Kigali. I was interviewing the "young pastor" who saw not only his entire family murdered, but nine thousand others as well.

We stood in lush green grass, dotted with yellow flowers, overhead was a clear blue sky. It was a beautiful spring day—a picture of peace.

The interpreter relayed the answers to my often-insensitive inquiries. I was dealing with hard facts, statistics, looking for a new way to tell a story that I had already heard too many times.

When I thought I had all the information that this young man could supply, I began to close my notebook. Certain that he could see I wanted this interview to end, I asked one final question—a throw-away question laced with more than the normal amount of doubt.

"These nine thousand, where are they buried?"

The interpreter paused, looked down at the ground as he relayed the question. The "young pastor" looked me straight in the eye, and without using the interpreter said with a choking voice, "You are standing on them."

Then it hit me. How stupid! Of course. The gentle slopes, the lush grass...so well fertilized. A wave of humiliation washed over me. *You stupid clod. And you call yourself perceptive.*

Somehow, I had forgotten that this really happened to real people. Men, women, children who died, not in groups of nine thousand, but one at a time.

I knelt on one knee and plucked one of the yellow flowers. I knew that if I stuck my finger into the red clay I would feel the remains of those buried there.

The flower has lost its color, but not its significance. It reminds me to dig deeper, to attempt to ask "why," and to search for a way to break the cycle of violence.

The answer, like the problem, can be "told," but it must go beyond the "reaches of journalism."

Who Is to Blame? Root Causes

For My people are foolish,
They have not known Me.
They are silly children,
And they have no understanding.
They are wise to do evil,
But to do good they have no knowledge
(Jeremiah 4:22).

In a discussion of "what happened" to any country in Africa, Rwanda being no exception, three views surface. Each considers a different factor to be the element responsible for what happened.

The first is **ethnicity,** formerly called "tribal warfare." This view stresses the fact that most Rwandans are from one of two tribes, the Hutu and the Tutsi. It is pointed out that for several centuries the Tutsis played the role of lording over the Hutus. "Without question," this view points out, "there were indeed ethnic inequalities in pre-colonial Rwanda, with the Tutsis subjugating the Hutus, but it was a benevolent relationship that both accepted."

Proponents of this view suggest that these pre-colonial inequalities were carried on into the colonial period, which compounded the inequalities, and "today's conflict is an attempt to redress the imbalance as perceived by each tribe."

Those who give less credence to this view point out that ethnicity by any definition still means desire for raw power over others. That is what motivates both Hutus and Tutsis. Rwanda is not alone in this world in which ethnicity, or "the color of one's skin," is used by corrupt and overly ambitious leadership as an excuse to gain personal power. No progress can be made until this issue is dealt with. Ignoring this issue only perpetuates the problem and leads to open, and often deadly, conflict.

Ethnicity, however, should be less of an issue in Rwanda than in other sub-Saharan governments. Scholars point out that Rwanda is unique among other African nations, in that the Hutus and Tutsis share not only a common language, but a common culture, history, and religion. All of which should diminish the problem of ethnicity or tribal conflict.

The second factor that must be examined before one can proceed to discuss cause and effect is **colonialism.** Those viewing this factor as the predominate element in the equation deny any "pre-colonial inequalities." They blame the colonial regime itself—in the case of Rwanda, the Belgians—for having been the architects of a scheme that has severely disrupted the supposedly peaceful coexistence of the sub-groups. They agree that the Hutus and Tutsis share a common heritage, but the equilibrium was disrupted by the coming of colonialism.

They point out that the only real distinction between the two groups is their mode of life, which has a lot to do with their subsistence. The Hutus raise crops, while the Tutsis raise cattle; but both "live side by side with their own role to play." This assumes that the Hutus like being dominated, a point with which the Hutus would vehemently disagree. The Tutsis, on the other hand, point out that the Hutus were grateful for the protection given them by their warrior landlords.

Proponents who view colonialism as the primary source of conflict point out that the colonial scheme of deliberate "divide and conquer" created the sharp division that led to the present conflict.

The last of the three factors, and certainly the most relevant and provable, is **leadership.** In Rwanda specifically, but in other sub-Saharan governments as well, postcolonial leadership has been less than successful (and too often catastrophic). The Hutu-dominated Habyarimana regime, though moderate in many ways, was unfortunately not a notable exception. It also attempted to explain away obvious abuses listing all sorts of sectarian sentiments as fundamental causes while ignoring the real causes: ineptness, corruption, and tribal prejudices.

One example used is the introduction of a required identity card identifying one's ethnicity, which in turn determined access to employment, education, marital prospects, and other aspects of daily life.

Of these three factors or causes, the problem of leadership is most critical. It involves the present. If the last thirty years' leadership example is followed, the future is not very bright.

George B. N. Ayittey, professor of economics at American University in Washington, D.C., himself an African-American and author of *Africa Betrayed*[1], gives an important analysis of the leadership problem.

The disenchantment of the African people with their leaders began much earlier—in the 1960s. There was no question that colonial injustices were perpetrated against the African people. But the leadership that assumed power after independence continued with the same denigration and oppression of the African people. It was all the more painful when the atrocities were being committed by the very leaders who claimed to have brought freedom to Africa. Some freedom.

Those who won their countries' first elections subsequently transformed themselves into "life presidents." "Power to the People!" these leaders chanted. But they declared themselves "presidents for life," refusing to give their people the real power to remove them. "Colonialism was oppressive and raped Africa of its resources!" Of course, these leaders never saw the oppression they were meting out against their own people. In addition, they looted Africa's wealth for deposit in Swiss bank accounts while their own people starved. How were these leaders different from the colonialists? Name one indigenous African chief who had such an account. "Apartheid is evil!" African leaders rightly asserted. But they never looked to see where they were standing—on the necks of their own people. These leaders turned the office of the presidency into their own personal property. Any attempt to remove them from power for incompetence was derided as "an imperialist/neocolonial plot."

Ask these leaders about the causes of Africa's problems and they will wax eloquent on colonialism, American imperialism, the pernicious effects of slavery, the unjust international economic system, and exploitation by multinational corporations. Of course, they will never mention their own incompetence and pursuance of wrong-headed policies. Obviously, without a proper diagnosis black African problems cannot be solved.

Black African leaders constantly complain about these problems but disgracefully cannot take the initiative on their own, expecting somebody else— either the government or some foreign charitable organization—to come and solve them.

Aiya-Obs, an African living in Los Angeles, admonished, "We as black people have to accept our challenges and abandon excuses and white scapegoating for our lack of gut to venture into the unknown" (*West Africa*, 14–20 May 1990, 816). Ariz L. Issarrah of Accra added his voice: "It seems to me as though we the black society have the tendency to complain more than to act" (*West Africa*, 20–26 May 1991, 788).

What kind of sub-Saharan Africa has this modern, post-colonial leadership given us? The picture is dark. The decline in the living standards of sub-Saharan Africa, that traditional part of Africa that extends from the Arab world to South Africa, is painfully obvious.

You don't have to be an expert in nation building to be moved to compassion by so much potential gone awry. You see it in the fly-infested corridors of hospitals where disease flourishes, the empty classrooms, the broken-down infrastructure, the mismanagement and corruption. What used to be "one country at a time" despair is now shared or about to be shared by most, if not all, of Rwanda's neighbors.

More than four million African children born this year

will die before the age of five. Nearly one-third of the children are at this moment malnourished and prime targets for disease. One child in three goes without a primary school education. The population growth rate of 3.2 percent is the highest in the world. The economy is not keeping up with the population growth; in fact it is consistently falling behind.

Food production is down 20 percent from twenty-five years ago. Food producers are immigrating to the big cities in search of "new beginnings."

It is a vicious cycle that is going to take more than discussion of "root causes" to break. Mismanagement, corruption, a crumbling infrastructure, repressive political climates must all be faced and tackled. Leadership must be held responsible.

Before moving on, there is one "root cause" that is not often discussed but is tremendously relevant, and that is the **handling of crisis**[2], whether it be in Rwanda, Somalia, Nigeria, Angola, or Zaire.

The crisis explodes, the world press arrives, the UN holds a meeting, non-governmental organizations supply temporary relief, and after a respectable period of participation everyone packs up and heads for the next crisis.

A crisis handled strictly by the wisdom of man inevitably turns into a disaster, and in the case of Africa, not just a continuing but a contagious disaster.

The simple concept of giving food, medical supplies, and money too often plays into the hands of corrupt leadership.

David Keen, a research officer at Oxford University, has written a book, *The Benefits of Famine*[3]. He recently addressed the subject in an op-ed article of *The New York*

Times. It makes very sober reading.

Ten years after the Ethiopian disaster comes the Rwanda catastrophe, and evidence, if it was needed, that Africa[4] has still not shaken the sickness of violence and famine. The vast growth of spending on emergency relief has neither addressed the causes of humanitarian disaster nor ensures effective aid for their victims. Probably nothing will change either, until the world acknowledges that wars and famine are typically manipulated in a rational—if immoral—manner by those who expect to benefit from it....

Assaults on the food supply have become a key military strategy in Africa's civil rebel movements of recruits, support and civilian cover by destroying local economies and forcing the exodus of civilians.... With government and rebels competing for control of the people, the international agencies' habitual pleas that relief be "politically neutral" have repeatedly fallen on deaf ears.

Keen then points out examples such as Ethiopia where "Tigre, the worst hit province, with a third of the affected population, received only 5 percent of the relief food. It was no coincidence that Tigre was a rebel stronghold."

Keen states:

In many African civil wars, raids on livestock and grain have provided sustenance for poorly paid soldiers and unpaid militias including those allied with the rebel movement. At the root of the famine in Sudan were raids by impoverished northern herders on the southern Dinka, seen as key rebel supporters. The government, unable to afford a large standing army, provided the militia with arms, information, encouragement, and effective legal immunity [as wages for their services, i.e., killing the enemy].

In Rwanda, government responsibility for attacks on civilians was disguised as "tribal anarchy."...

The resulting famine caused alarming death rates. But it had its winners—including the traders and army officers who helped finance and organize the raids. Selling expensive grain and buying cheap cattle they restricted flows of grain to the famine region. Some farmers have even used migrants as slaves.

"The benefits of famines can also include access to diverted relief," says Keen, pointing out that in Somalia, extracting relief and protection money from aid agencies became big business. In Ethiopia, Sudan, and Mozambique, relief became a key source of foreign currency to help finance war.

More to the point, Keen reports that "Rwandan Hutu extremists are apparently hoping to regain their power base by cajoling refugees to stay in Zaire and by manipulating international aid."

It is this kind of sub-Saharan Africa, Rwanda included, that we find today. Obviously our "crisis" has turned into a "disaster." Though we appreciate the "goodness of man" to help feed the starving and clothe the naked, it is at best only temporary help, and in some cases, part of the problem. We obviously need more insight.

Rwanda must now rise above that mentality, admit that terrible injustices have indeed existed, perpetuated by the colonialists and their own people, and then move on. Few times in African history has there been such a need and opportunity for a light of truth to penetrate the darkness of the past, and to create a society that truly "walks in the light."

1 George B. N. Ahittey, *Africa Betrayed* (St. Martin Press, 1992). This is a rare book on Africa, and should be read by anyone seriously concerned with the future of that continent.

2 This subject will be dealt with in greater detail in a later chapter.

3 David Keen, "Violence and famines government–inspired?" *The New York Times*, 17 August 1994. This problem is illustrated in detail in the author's book, *The Benefits of Famine* (Oxford University, 1994).

4 Though Keen is dealing with all of Africa, his comments apply primarily to the sub-Sahara area.

Rebuilding

All your enemies have opened their mouth against you;
They hiss and gnash their teeth.
They say, "We have swallowed her up!
Surely this is the day we have waited for..."
(Lamentations 2:16).

The rebuilding of Rwanda is a task that is as urgent as it is monumental. Seventy-four percent of the population remains displaced. The sorghum and bean fields are taken over by wild grass. The remains of what were thriving businesses are now unoccupied shells. The walls of homes that used to echo with the laughter of children and the bustle of housewives are now pitted with bullet holes. The schoolyards where children once played and the church-yards where their parents once prayed are now graveyards.

Kigali, the capital, used to have 300,000 inhabitants. UN officials say one-third are now dead and many others remain in refugee camps. Many new inhabitants of the city are the former exiles who have returned behind the RPF army. They have simply taken over vacant houses and buildings and started rebuilding. The marketplaces, once crowded with tomatoes, beans, and goat meat, are slowly reviving. In the center of the city on the Avenue la Justice, someone has planted a bean field.

Any consideration of rebuilding has to give serious thought to those in the refugee camps, where two million people are subsisting at nearly sub-human levels.

Despite repeated attempts and pleas by the new government and humanitarian organizations, the refugees fear that if they attempt to go home they will be killed. Yet, if they stay they may die of disease. They are virtually being held prisoners by their former executioners, the Hutus, who followed the survivors of their massacres into camps for safety as the RPF reclaimed Rwanda.

The new government realizes that every day two things are happening that make rebuilding more difficult, if not impossible. First, the exiles and survivors who remained in the country are taking possession of more and more of the houses, businesses, and farmland, so when the refugees return they may well be homeless. Second, with each day that passes, the Hutus in refugee camps and in exile are training and building a growing dedicated army whose sole purpose is to continue the job started a year ago: Kill the Tutsis. Reports indicate they are being supplied arms by other countries. Hutu power has no lack of resources of its own, having fled into exile with all the funds in the Bank of Rwanda, which included $100,000,000 in gold reserves.

Donor nations are beginning to balk at the idea of feeding and sheltering these Hutu warriors and suspected killers in their midst.

The U.S. assistant secretary of state, after visiting one of the camps where two thousand people were massacred when they tried to leave, admits to a helpless feeling. "We are aware of the moral dilemma and none of us have the means to solve it."

A director of an aid agency is less diplomatic, "We have botched the job and are now at a loss as to how to fix it."

The UN tells anyone who will listen that "hundreds, perhaps thousands of the suspected killers are working in the camps—paid from our funds—as engineers, medical workers, latrine diggers, drivers, and other staff laborers which are needed to keep the camps operating."

The new Rwandan government has asked that all suspected "war criminals be returned from the camps to Kigali to face war crime charges." As suspects in the camp are identified, they cannot be removed, for in minutes the Hutus summon a mob of refugees to protest. The officials, fearing violence, leave, and the protesters line up to get their extra food ration, which just happens to be controlled by the former executioners.

Those who work for the humanitarian organizations feel the dilemma the most. One puts it: "Daily we face the question of whether or not we are to help those very ones who bludgeoned, hacked, burned, or shot to death unarmed men, women and children and now hold the survivors of that massacre captive in these so-called refugee camps."

One refugee cried out, "We are caught between two deaths. Yesterday I wrapped the body of my ten-year-old daughter in the only piece of cloth we had, and carried her out to the roadside and laid her on the pile for the trucks to pick her up and take her to a mass grave." His other four children, caked with dirt, no longer able to smile, all hope drained from their young souls, sat beside him on a straw mat, one of the few possessions he has left. His fear is that even that mat will be gone tomorrow, as he will use it to wrap his sick wife, lying nearby, and carry her to the roadside as well.

Another family weighs the consequences of choosing between two deaths. It is not a choice that anyone wants to make, but it is being forced upon them as the vicious cycle continues—one group trying to increase its power and the other trying to regain what it has lost.

In the end it has little to do with one's tribe, but much to do about the satanic hunger for raw power—disguised as ethnicity.

"Her adversaries have become the master, her enemies prosper..." (Lamentations 1:5).

Reconciliation and Justice

No more shall every man teach his neighbor,
and every man his brother,
saying, "Know the LORD," for they all shall know Me,
from the least of them to the greatest of them, says the LORD.
For I will forgive their iniquity,
and their sin I will remember no more
(Jeremiah 31:34).

Eyes burn with hate, fists are clenches, as they enunciate a feeling that has been burning inside their mouths for months. They spit out the words, "They killed my wife and children, right here, right in front of me. They left me for dead and walked away laughing. And you expect me to forgive them?" The fist is raised as if making a pledge to the heavens, "Never, never, never!"

Reconciliation, defined as "the restoration of friendship and harmony," faces some formidable barriers. As one survivor put it, "Too many people have been destroyed. The living cannot forget the dead even if they wanted to. We must live to repay."

The survivors of the Rwandan massacre seem more bent on revenge than reconciliation. Any road to "harmony and friendship" seems as encumbered with road blocks as the paths leading out of the refugee camps. It will take a special miracle for either road to open.

There is, however, an honest effort being made by the new Tutsi–run Rwandan Patriotic Front to bring about a beginning to the reconciliation process. They have appointed some Hutus to key positions, they have vowed to avoid references to Rwanda's ethnic groups in announcements or literature, and they have promised to add courses on ethnic tolerance to school curricula to be used when schools reopen.

Gaining power as they have by military means, they are making concerted efforts to merge the two warring factions by bringing Hutu soldiers into the Tutsi-dominated RPF Army. A military camp has been set aside for "harmonization training." Two thousand officers and soldiers of the former Hutu army, minus the "militia," are being brought together in classes and discussion groups. The curriculum centers around being Rwandans, not Hutus or Tutsis. The message may be simple, but it cannot be stressed enough to a vanquished army where most participated in massacres or did little to stop them. The classes range from military drills to debates on political systems of government. The second-in-command explains that "we discuss and compare our philosophy with the former regime. As time goes on, I hope we shall make it."

However, building a national army where ethnicity does not matter can only be effectual if it can accommodate the thousands of Hutu soldiers of the former extremist government that are in the refugee camps. Getting them back into the country is seen as a critical factor on which so much of the future hinges. The longer the "militia" stays in the camps, the more time they have to develop into a guerrilla-army-in-exile. Even for soldiers who have no blood on their hands, the road to reconciliation is long, filled with pot holes of humility, abnegation, pride, and of course, hate.

The participants of this "harmonization" program have serious doubts as to whether or not it will work, or that they will ever be accepted as equals by their former enemies once they are integrated. In their words: "To put two people who hate each other into the same uniform does not change the inside of either man. In a moment he can tear the uniform off and go to war, naked, if need be."

The government itself is having some problems with defining just what it means by "reconciliation." In their weekly newspaper the headline reads, "National Reconciliation and the Legacy of Genocide."[1] The story goes on, "The lines of reconciliation have yet to be drawn. Will the Rwandan people reconcile with all those who planned or helped plan and carry out the genocide in Rwanda? Can you reconcile with someone who macheted your children or your parents?"

At least publicly the new government is committed to what it calls a policy of "reconciliation."

At the center of the movement are plans to bring to justice in a court of law those who have committed crimes against their fellow Rwandans. The official paper states:

> The first grain of any belief in reconciliation lies in
> an exhaustive effort to bring to books and punish all
> those who planned or carried out the genocide. The
> Rwandan people would like to know and see that
> the culture of committing atrocities with impunity
> has come to an end in their country. This will

ensure that justice has been seen to be done, and it will enhance hope for national reconciliation. If justice is done, the survivors will nurse no grudges, but if the killers remain at large, no one would feel safe and the bereaved might justifiably seek revenge.

One should note the word "reconciliation" seems to be synonymous with "revenge," and lacks any concept of "forgiveness."

No one doubts that what happened in Rwanda was bonafide genocide. As much as some have whitewashed it and defined it as a recurring problem of "ethnic cleansing" the fact remains that it fulfills all the elements of genocide as set down by international law, which defines genocide as:

killing on a massive scale or...other acts committed with intent to destroy, in whole or part, a national ethnic or religious group. Such crimes against humanity may include murder, extermination, enslavement, deprivation, imprisonment, torture, rape, political, racial and religious persecution and other inhumane acts, when such acts are committed as part of a systematic attack against the civilian population.

The problem is not in the definition, but in the fulfilling of the act of "justice."

The Rwandan government started rounding up Hutu "suspects" in August of 1994. Eight hundred suspected perpetrators of the genocide were arrested. This number has now increased to about 23,000. There are credible reports that up to one hundred persons are being arrested daily.

Where do they keep them all? Some prisoners, including women and children, are crowded into open-air prison compounds. Undoubtedly many of those arrested are innocent.

Of genuine concern is how the police gather incriminating information. If a Tutsi returned to Kigali or to his farm or village and found a vacant house, he simply took possession. The same is true of business sites. If the legal Hutu owner returns from a camp or exile and demands the return of his property, it is a rather simple matter to go to the police and say, "So-and-so has returned. I saw him kill So-and-so. He must be arrested." Very often he is. This is where revenge, joined by greed, makes reconciliation an almost impossible dream.

Often innocent returnees are arrested on sheer hearsay, or the agreement of a friendly witness. The accused are taken to an overcrowded prison that can lead to poor health, perhaps death, but probably never "reconciliation," even if they might eventually be declared innocent.

Amnesty International, a human rights organization, reported recently[2] that "seven or more detainees were dying daily in the Kigali prison." The prison currently holds 5,162. It was designed to hold 1,500. Butuare prison has a capacity of 1,500 but currently holds 4,122, including eighty-five women, thirty-five minors, and around twenty-two infants (with their mothers). Some prisoners are held in private houses and military barracks, where humanitarian agencies have no access. Reports are that detainees have "generally little food, and medical care is inadequate and sporadic."

Adding to the horror is the question of how long detainees will have to stay in prison before they receive a trial.

A judicial system in Rwanda hardly exists. Only two hundred of the eight hundred former magistrates employed by the Rwandan government before April 1994 survived the massacres. About 5 percent have formal legal training. There are fewer than twelve prosecutors and thirty-six criminal investigators in the entire country. Justice is going to be a long time in coming.

In the meantime, false accusations continue. There have been a few trials for the sake of the press, but thousands still languish in nearly sub-human conditions in prisons, barracks, and private homes with very little hope, as Hutus become victims of Tutsis.

A typical example of the "new victims" of a nation turning on itself is Jospehone Mukanyangezi. She is a former judge and a widow with two children. She was arrested on September 5, 1994, by two members of the armed forces who she claims had no official documents authorizing an arrest. She has never heard who her accusers are or what the evidence might be.

One of the arresting officers told her that his relative had been killed by her brother. They accused her of being in charge of military groups responsible for killing Tutsi families during the genocide. She was taken to a house in which one of the officers had taken up residence. The owners of the house had fled during the war. She was locked up with her two children in a pit latrine (a small room with a hole in the ground) for three days and nights. A leaking car battery was being stored in the latrine. She and her children were forced to sit in the battery acid that covered the floor. She has burn scars on her legs as a result. She was denied food and water and was badly beaten. She is currently being held in Kigali Central prison and has not yet been charged.

Her children are being looked after by a friend. Her father died in custody in January 1995. Her two brothers are in exile, fearing, because of their sister's position, a similar fate if they return. Her story is repeated often in refugee and exile camps.

One would hope that a nation professing to be 80 percent Christian would have a better understanding of "reconciliation." Until they do, one can only weep with those who weep, as they see the deadly practice of genocide preparing to be recycled on the innocent people of Rwanda.

1*Rwanda Weekly*, Vol. 1, No. 0001, April 1995, 1,3
2"Rwanda Crying Out for Justice," *Amnesty International*, April 1995. AL INDIX:AFR 47/03/95

Damocles Sword, Hanging by a Thread

Remember, O LORD, what has come upon us;
Look, and behold our reproach!
We have become orphans and waifs,
our mothers are like widows.
You, O LORD, remain forever;
Your throne from generation to generation
(Lamentations 5:1,3,19).

Reconciliation is only one of the problems hanging over the head of Rwanda and much of sub-Sahara Africa, like Damocles's sword. Another foreboding shadow is being cast by AIDS.

While driving through Rwanda's neighbor country, Uganda, it is not uncommon to see several people sitting under a tree, dying of AIDS. They have nowhere to go. There are entire villages where the only survivors of the AIDS epidemic are children and the very old.

In Kigali, the capital of Rwanda, in 1992, 60 percent of all hospital patients were HIV positive. New statistics are no longer available since foreign Human Rights organizations have convinced the government that to report or even test for AIDS without the patient's permission is a violation of that person's rights.

One difference between Africa and some other continents is that here AIDS is spread largely through heterosexual contact. The most recent figures show that of the more than fourteen million people in the world who have been infected with the HIV virus, about nine million are in sub-Saharan Africa, which includes Rwanda. In some hospitals an estimated 60 to 70 percent of the beds are filled with AIDS patients. The epidemic robs countries of what should be their most productive age group.

It has taken seventy-five years for another epidemic, tuberculosis, to reach its apex in Africa. First identified in 1908, it reached that apex in 1985. What worries doctors is that TB and AIDS are now on a collision course, and TB is not going down, but increasing. Estimates are that 80 percent of new TB cases are HIV positive and that 60 percent of all persons infected with the virus will die in the next two years from TB, the opportunistic disease of nature's choice.

A medical doctor in one refugee camp who specializes in virulent diseases (especially AIDS) told me it would be rather conservative to say that about 75 percent of the more than 300,000 inhabitants of that camp are now, or soon will be, HIV positive.

Of the women who are HIV positive and giving birth to children, one quarter of those children are HIV positive. This means that in a couple of years both the mother and the child will probably succumb to the disease.

However, of the other 75 percent of the children, the mother will eventually die of AIDS, being HIV positive, while the child, being HIV negative, will become an orphan.

The UN estimates that there are at least 100,000 "unaccompanied children" roaming the countryside in small bands, living in the streets, or in orphanages. They are called "unaccompanied" until such time as they can verify that their parents are deceased.

To this must be added a problem that is the direct result of the present conflict. During their rampage, the Hutus raped many women. It is estimated that those rape victims have now, or are in the process of giving birth to forty thousand children that they call "snakes in their belly." These children are not wanted, consequently they are abandoned when they are born. Again, the most notable victims are the children.

The new Tutsi-controlled government does not want these children to be adopted outside their own country, and have also informed foreign humanitarian agencies that they want to run all the orphanages. Why? The RPF army is aware that it is made up of children of Tutsi exiles, and they realize the importance of being in control of the raising of these children, understanding each one is a potential RPF soldier.

These two problems, added to the others, make us realize that man is rarely able to assuage the grief he creates. However heroic the effort may be at nation rebuilding, the answer is obviously not in the oft-tried schemes of man. We need to look for a better answer.

Questions That Need Answers

"Will You surely be to me like an unreliable stream,
as waters that fail?"
Therefore thus says, the LORD:
"If you return, then I will bring you back;
You shall stand before Me;
If you take out the precious from the vile,
You shall be as My mouth.
Let them return to you, but you must not return to them.
And I will make you to this people a fortified bronze wall;
And they will fight against you,
but they shall not prevail against you;
For I am with you to save you and deliver you," says the LORD.
"I will deliver you from the hand of the wicked,
And I will redeem you from the grip of the terrible"
(Jeremiah 15:18b–21).

To observe first hand a tragedy as apocalyptic as Rwanda's often creates a questioning of one's most sacred beliefs. There are many more questions than there are answers. That is what took me back to Rwanda a second time—to search for answers to these haunting and vexing questions.

The first question sets a framework for the others. **How is Rwanda's situation today different from a year ago?**

Last year, in April and May of 1994, bodies were seen lying beside the road, some having been dead only a few hours.

Now, a year later, on that same road is a lone combat boot protruding from under a bush. Upon close examination, a leg bone is seen sticking out of the boot, still attached to the foot inside.

Last year the Hutu-controlled radio was a cacophony of militant exhortations such as "If Tutsis must die, let them die." The militia constantly threatened non-militant Hutus, "If we don't see the blood of a Tutsi on your machete, we will see that it is covered with your blood."

Today, indigenous music is interspersed with European classics as the announcer steadily and calmly reminds people, "We do not want revenge. We must have justice and then reconciliation." The Tutsi listener responds, "Wait. They killed my wife and my children and left me for dead, nearly hacked to death with their machetes. You want me to forgive them. Never, never...not until the last Hutu is dead."

A year ago the people seemed to be in shock, fear etched on their faces.

Today there is an outward determination to get on with life, while the countenance appears more haunted, questioning "why," and fearing "it will happen again."

A year ago the fearful were running for a safe haven,

single-mindedly focused on survival, pushing aside anything in their way, sometimes trampling the children and infirm.

Today the gait is slower, pensive while searching for the face of a loved one that has disappeared, all the while fearing the loved one was one of the million mowed down by fear.

Last year's demonic, glass-eyed militia, drunk with their own power, has been replaced by the resolute stance of the RPF, determined that "this time we will not run."

The second question is more difficult. **What happened?**

U.S. News & World Report correspondent, Eric Ransdell, in the conclusion to a very insightful article[1] on Rwanda, gives one answer to that question. He writes:

> At its heart, Rwanda's tragedy was essentially a local drama. What distinguished its corrupt rulers from other Third World autocrats wasn't their lust for power but their ability to manipulate age old ethnic tensions and transform their largely uneducated population into a nation of murderers.
>
> The tragedy takes on a larger meaning in a new changed world where corrupt dictators and entrenched elites view democracy as an invention of mankind for the disenfranchisement of the powerful in favor of the weak.

The truth of Ransdell's words are sharpened and refined by the words of U.S. Ambassador, David Rawson, in response to the question, "What happened?"

We underestimated the power of evil. The devil is a

roaring lion. Evil here in Rwanda is not some personal little matter like a headache. Our prayer [life] must be more than, "Lord, cure my migraine."...

Evil, here in Rwanda as in all the world, is an incredibly destructive force. The U.S. is not protected. We have to realize how fragile is the fabric of society, any society. When any of us begin to diminish the importance of a neighbor's humanity, we are on a slippery slope.

When it becomes more important for me to survive than for someone else, then I am in trouble. It is possible that it is at that point I must choose not whom I will serve, which is myself, but whom I will kill. After all, I tell myself, it is better I live than another, so that I might continue to serve the Lord.

Then there is the third question, the most haunting of the three. Rwanda is reportedly one of the most Christian of nations in Africa. Statistics are that 80 percent of the people profess to be Christians. If, in a population of what was then more than eight million people, up to one million of them were massacred, then at least statistically there had to be Christians killing Christians. **Did Christians kill other Christians?**

First, we have to consider that statistic of 80 percent. Mark Twain said there were three kinds of lies: "lies, damnable lies, and statistics." This statistic falls into that category. We chuckle at the phrase, "evangelistically speaking," but it's no joke. Too often people zealous for "results" measure church growth with a rubber yardstick. Eighty percent of the Rwandan people may say they are Christians, but it would appear that a much smaller number have, in reality, gone beyond that statistical "raised hand" count. It is a "damnable lie" that may look good on a visiting evangelist's newsletter to his constituents back in America, but it is devastating to the whole concept of what it really means to be a part of God's kingdom.

Putting aside statistics, the question remains, did Christians kill Christians? Was the church part and parcel of this tragedy?

Pastor Antoine Rostatiyra, whose expertise is not in statistics, but in Christian reconciliation, points out:

> We must indeed blame the church for what happened in that they saw it coming and did nothing about it. The church supported the ethnic equilibrium, and even let it come into the church. The Bishop was picked not for his understanding of what God wanted for Rwanda, but for "the size of his nose." Though the Bishops knew many Tutsis who were in exile, they made no move to bring them back, to accept them as brothers. They consistently sided with the ruling party, the Hutus, and left the Tutsis to brood and train in exile.

Antoine suggests that "the church of Rwanda married the government, a marriage that was proposed in 1942 when the king supposedly became a Christian and was baptized. Regretfully, all his subjects then became Christian as well, and took baptism"—and became part of the 80 percent!

As Constantine did no favor for Christianity by declaring Christianity a state religion, so the king's baptism only hurt the church.

In 1959 the king became a threat to Belgian rule. Though not ill, he was encouraged to have a medical checkup, and he subsequently died. Rumor has it that he was poisoned. The Belgians had rid themselves of their pox.

"After that, the church walked in step with the government," according to Antoine. "They saw things through the eyes of politicians, who happened to be Hutus."

Antoine asserts:

Other problems that brought the church to where it was before the massacre are attributed to the fact that during the great revivals of 1930, the church rightly attacked moral issues: theft, drunkenness, adultery, jealousy...[but] all at the expense of social issues. Social problems were considered to be out of the sphere of God's grace.

The presentation of the Gospel was unbalanced. Both moral and social issues needed to be addressed. There can be little doubt that the church must share some of the blame for recent events.

However, as to the question of whether Christians took part in the killings, Antoine stresses, "There is a vast difference between being killed *in* a church, and being killed *by* the church."

One has to consider that starting with the first massacre in 1958, and several after that, the churches were always safe sanctuaries. It was the one safe place where people could go until the fighting ended and would then quietly return to their homes, unmolested. This time it was different. The church became a major target. Many of those massacred in the churches were not members of the church however, or even professing Christians, and it is a credit to the church that it had a reputation for being a sanctuary where people could find safety.

"However," says Antoine, "Christians may not have killed Christian but regretfully, some who called themselves Christian did participate by not attempting to do what they could to stay the massacres."

That answer brings up another question. **How did the Church** (not the so-called 80 percent, but that unmeasurable remnant who not only accepted Jesus Christ as Savior, but as Lord of their lives) **respond to the invasion of their sanctuaries?**

Verifiable stories of their actions could easily add another chapter to *Fox's Book of Martyrs.*

More than two hundred people sought sanctuary in a local church. The Hutu militia came and called them outside. As they gathered men, women and children, the militia leader told all the Hutus to separate themselves from the Tutsis and step to one side. Everyone knew what would happen; as soon as this was done there would be the staccato of AK–47s, the blast of hand grenades, the glare of striking machetes, after which the Hutus would be free to return to the sanctuary.

As if each of them were instructed by an inner voice, all of them, Hutus and Tutsis, moved as one to the side. The militia became frustrated and told them they misunderstood, Hutus were to separate themselves. Again the order was given. "All Tutsis move back to where you were, and Hutus, stay where you are." Again, all moved as one.

The cursing of the militia leader was silenced by the pastor, himself a Hutu. He stepped forward and without animosity quietly told the militia leader, "We are neither Hutu or Tutsi. We are Christian. We are all brothers in the Lord Jesus Christ."

A holy silence was shattered by the sound of hot metal piercing the innocent bodies of men, women, and children, followed by the hacking sounds of glittering pieces of metal against non-resistant human flesh. And then silence again. The church had given a powerful, and final, message.

In another church of several hundred, the militia ordered all the Hutus to leave the church building. No one left. The pastor gave the same simple response to their request, "In Jesus Christ we are neither Hutus nor Tutsis. We are brothers in the Lord Jesus Christ." It was the benediction for both the shepherd and his flock.

Two women, one elderly Hutu and a young Tutsi mother of several children, spent time together every day praying. One day the Hutu woman told her younger Tutsi friend about a strange dream she'd had two nights in a row. In the dream, she was told that God would give her children. Though taken seriously, they still laughed at the idea of this elderly woman, whose family was grown, being capable of having more children.

The militia came. The Tutsis were having a prayer meeting. It ended suddenly. Hearing what was happening the elderly woman ran to help but was too late. Eighteen Tutsis lay dead. As she stood in disbelief at the carnage, the old woman heard a whimper. Attempting to crawl out from under the body of the woman's young Tutsi friend was her youngest child. Remembering the dream, the old lady picked up the child. She had a family again.

In the confusion of trying to evade bullets and hand

grenades, a family was separated. The five children took refuge in a church with other people. While their parents looked for them, the Hutus came to that church. Two days later the parents found their five children. In the hands of one was a letter to the parents. It read, "We know we are going to die, but don't let anyone avenge our death. God is our avenger." They buried their children and hugged the letter to their breast, vowing they would fulfill it to the letter. No revenge would come from this family.

A Hutu Christian, a captain in the regular army, now under the direction of the militia was driving a military pickup from one checkpoint to another when he came across a group of about twenty Tutsis, mostly young people, running toward what they hoped would be a place of safety. The young Hutu captain knew of a back road, so told them to get on board and he would drive them to safety. Unknown to him a new militia checkpoint had been established along this route. When he came to it, the militia, assuming the captain was delivering a human cargo of escapees, ordered the Tutsis to get out of the pickup and line up. The captain jumped out of the pickup shouting that they were his prisoners and he was the one responsible for them. He was transported to eternal safety with his young cargo; their vehicle was death. Later one of the militia present at the scene confessed he was a Christian and would carry guilt and remorse the rest of his life for not standing beside the captain and his passengers so that he could have died with them.

A missionary reports he saw several young Hutu men put their arms around their Tutsi friends and tell the militia, "We are ready to die, just give us a moment to pray together." It was of necessity a very short prayer.

A believer with a glow of joy on her face tells how "it was so wonderful of the Lord that my friends died from the machete rather than the guns, because it gave them time to repent"—while they were slowly being hacked to death.

Forget "80 percent." The answer is clear. I heard of no verifiable cases of believers in Jesus Christ killing other believers. The sick feeling that haunted me for a year, after visiting the refugee camps in 1994, has now been replaced by shame that I would have even thought it was so in the first place. The church in Rwanda has written one of the most inspiring chapters in the entire history of the Christian movement in Africa. No, true believers did not kill fellow Christians. Another of the Lord's great promises has been fulfilled: "I will build My church, and the gates of Hades [machine guns, hand grenades, and machetes of the militia] shall not prevail against it" (Matthew 16:18).

1Article by Eric Ransdell, *U.S. News & World Report*, 28 November 1994, 74.

The Church Today

And who is a chosen man that I may appoint over her?
For who is like Me?
Who will arraign Me?
And who is that shepherd who will withstand Me?
(Jeremiah 49:19b).

As is often the case, when you answer one question to your satisfaction, the very answer poses another question. In this case, **what about the church today? How will it participate in the rebuilding process?**

Leadership is a problem because nearly 60 percent of the leading religious leaders—bishops, superintendents, etc.—are in exile. As Antoine puts it, "Their chair is occupied but empty." If they come back we may conclude that their near marriage to the former government would be a hindrance to reconciliation.

At the grassroots level, many of the pastors have either been killed or are in refugee camps. The good news is that these camps may serve as schools of evangelism and discipleship, creating new leaders for a later date.

During the massacres, missionaries met in Tanzania and pooled their resources so as not to overlap in their efforts. The *Haven of Rest* radio ministry purchased large tents for the camps to be used as points of evangelism and discipleship. Reportedly, they are extremely effective as the Rwandan pastors have a meeting place where people can come for teaching and evangelism. As the refugees slowly trickle back to their country, hopefully they will take with them what they have learned. The tents may be dismantled and transplanted in Rwanda, along with the principles of evangelism and discipleship.

In Rwanda itself, a major problem is that about 60 percent of those attending churches are returned exiles. This should not be a problem, but if their ambitions are more political than spiritual it will feed a weakness that has been so harmful in the present experience. Though they may produce today's leaders, there is a good chance they could create tomorrow's church-in-exile.

There are, however, some very encouraging pockets of growth.

There is a genuine concern among the survivors that if there is to be a genuine reconciliation, which is the only thing that can sever this disastrous cycle that has nearly destroyed Rwanda, it will have to come from the lay leadership.

There are reports of pastors and lay people meeting on a regular basis, not talking about prayer, but praying; not preaching the need for reconciliation, but reconciling.

It would seem that many denominational barriers have diminished that in the past put severe restrictions on the movement of the Spirit. For the first time, Pentecostals, non–Pentecostals, and mainline traditionalists are realizing the need to set the example for the rest of the nation and are themselves reconciling and showing the rest of the people that, like those who died together, they are neither Anglican, Baptist, nor Pentecostal, but simply brothers and sisters in Christ.

It would be a giant step forward if each denomination would corporately confess that the war has not been limited to two political factions and the weaponry has been more than machetes and guns. Rather, they in fact have been engaged for years in a more subtle and more vicious type of war of words, beliefs, and denominationalism that contributed to the climate that erupted into a massacre.

One young pastor who returned from the camps is admonishing his fellow believers:

> Engage in prayer warfare and start being prophets. Confess where you have been wrong and warn people that if they do not repent they will only perpetuate the massacres. Be priest and prophets to your own people. Remember that deeds follow words. Reconcile amongst yourselves, confess to one another, and then take to the streets. Minister to the widow and orphans, to the Hutus and Tutsis. We may never again have an opportunity such as this, and we will pay a greater price than exile if we turn our back on it.

Understanding the problems that the church leadership faces, raises another question: **What about the missionaries?**

To set the groundwork, a review of the missionary movement may be helpful.

Africa is often, and correctly, called the "white man's graveyard." More missionaries have died while serving there than on any other continent. In the late-nineteenth and early-twentieth centuries, only one out of four missionaries survived their first terms. Their commitment to their Lord gave more than lip service to the belief that the growth of the church of our Lord Jesus Christ is nurtured and watered by the blood of martyrs.

If success can be measured by the amount of resistance and criticism that one receives, then the success of the mission movement in Africa is spectacular indeed.

Missionaries in Africa have been regularly taken to task by both the Europeans and the Africans. In the colonial days they were accused by the Africans of being part and parcel of the colonial movement. In a sense, this was true. Many were there only because colonial powers permitted them to be. But the missionaries lived and died firmly believing and teaching that the Gospel was the very root of European culture. Their method may have been European, but their message was right from the heart of the Middle East.

The difference between the colonialists and missionaries was more defined when it came to slavery. Missionaries were always at the forefront of the anti-slavery movement. They were the first to demonstrate publicly in England against the heinous crime of trafficking in human cargo. Some historians now give them credit for putting so much pressure on the British government that it abolished slave trade in its own colonies.

However, the missionaries paid a heavy price. They were not only criticized, but despised by the Europeans. The colonialists maintained that there would be no slave trade if the Africans themselves were not willing to deliver up slaves to colonial ports. The missionaries argued that there would be no Africans selling their brothers or sisters to lives of slavery, if non-Africans weren't eager to purchase their human cargo.

The missionaries were also accused of being racists. This evolved from the fact that missionaries considered not only Africans, but all people who lacked the moral teaching and lifestyle of Jesus Christ, as "savages." The missionaries clashed head-on with the natives and helped bring an end to such practices as headhunting, cannibalism, human sacrifice, and other practices that even the colonialists thought of as pagan and self-destructive and terribly harmful to the Africans themselves.

Then, as now, however, the strongest critics were the Western social scientists and anthropologists. Like their counterparts today, they would accuse the missionaries, with their insistence on the need to follow Jesus Christ, of "wreaking havoc with local cultures."

One doubts that most of these intellectually elite have ever left their ivory-tower classrooms and their tenured palaces long enough to see the difference in the face of one held in bondage by the slavery of Satan and then delivered by the Gospel of Jesus Christ. Nor have they ever witnessed the suffering caused by practices no longer tolerated by African Christians. They've not felt the life-long pain inflicted on young girls by the ritual of female circumcision, performed by their grandmothers with the lid of a tin can.

Regarding the future and the rebuilding of a nation, **What kind of missionary is needed?**

Africa needs missionaries with *commitment* to God and His Church, missionaries that will say to their African brothers and sisters, "Wherever you go, I will go; and wherever you lodge, I will lodge. Your people shall be my people. And your God, my God. Where you die, I will die, and there I will be buried. The Lord do so to me, and more also, if anything but death part you from me."

Going to an unreached tribe or helping to build churches in cities like Kigali should not be a summer experiment (i.e., "I'll give it a try and if I like it, I'll return"). Africa needs a much deeper level of commitment than that.

What is commitment?

There is a pounding on the front gate. The rebels smash it down and head for your front door. You calmly open it and tell them, "Yes, I have some of them here, but I will not give them to you. They are my spiritual children and if you want to kill them, you will have to kill me first."

"Thank you for giving me warning, but I am not leaving. I realize that my citizenship gives me that right, but I came here not to live, if possible, but to die, if necessary. I will not leave the country. These are my people."

Such an example of commitment would be the most powerful and fruitful message a missionary could give.

You have every right to say to me, "Hey, wait a minute, that is easy for you to say, sitting in your comfortable basement office in Corvallis, Oregon, where your greatest danger is that a 'frat brat' may throw a beer can on your lawn." Nevertheless, the truth is: Africa's church needs missionaries with that kind of commitment.

Ron Hanson was saved at the age of seven. At a Billy Graham Crusade in Minneapolis, Minnesota, in 1949,

Graham asked all that wanted to commit their lives to missions to raise their hands. Ron did, and it was an act of commitment that followed him through his marriage to Gloria in 1956, his university training, and his job as a math teacher at a high school and junior college. He always told the Lord, in remembering that day at the Graham Crusade, "I'm available. You know where I am if you need me."

Then, one day in 1973, that pretext no longer worked. The Lord said, "Ron, you've been mouthing long enough. I want action."

A year later, as new missionaries, Ron and Gloria, with young sons Brent and Scott, arrived in Ethiopia. From there they would move to Nairobi and then Tanzania. Today Ron is an area director of relief for his church.

Their son Brent, now 26, has for several years been speaking to school children about AIDS. Recently in Malawi, in a period of six weeks, fourteen thousand students heard Brent tell them while pointing to his skin, "I am an American outside," then pointing to his heart, "but in here I am an African." He then goes on to explain the moral, spiritual, and physical issues that are at stake for each of them.

Scott, a year younger than Brent, recently married Karen Davis, whose great-grandfather went to Africa as a missionary doctor in 1909. Her grandfather and father both spent their entire adult lives in Africa as missionaries. Scott and Debra plan to live with an "unreached tribe," a primitive tribe sixty kilometers from the nearest medical facility and a nine-hour drive from the first and only village in the area to have electricity.

This family is an example of the type of missionary that is needed in Africa.

More specifically, what about missionaries in Rwanda?

Ben and Darlene Odell have spent more than thirty years in the villages of Africa. They know how to live without any of the modern conveniences their supporters take for granted. They have experienced the pain of separation year after year as they sent their daughters off to boarding schools for months at a time.

Recently (with the children grown and married) the Odells were looking forward to a well-earned sabbatical and spending some time with their grandchildren in Oklahoma.

But they had mixed emotions. They had grown to love the African people. The villages had become their home. It was hard to leave.

Their mission director offered them another challenge. A team was needed to go to Rwanda, to help rebuild a country being torn apart by ethnic violence.

Ben and Darlene packed up their personal belongings. With only their suitcases at their sides, they watched everything else being loaded onto a truck for shipment to Kigali, Rwanda.

It would be a new language, a new people, but the same call.

Several months later they sat together in the middle of an unfurnished room in Kigali. Darlene sat on the only seat, a small ice chest. Ben placed his cup of coffee on the other piece of furniture, a folding card table. Occasional gun shots could be heard. The electricity had been off for hours.

This was the "Rwanda Team." There were no other volunteers.

Later their personal belongings would arrive, but not until they had been carefully inspected at customs, and agents took what they wanted. If the Odells were fortunate, they might be able to buy some of the belongings back at a local "swap" market. If not, they would live without them.

Darlene would later write: "We were overwhelmed by what we found in Rwanda. Torn by the look in the eyes of the Rwandans, questions kept surfacing. What are we doing here? Why did we leave the comfort and security of Kenya to come to this place? We volunteered as part of a 'team', but now we find out this is it. We are the team.

"Telephones were not working. The post office had no stamps, and the U.S. post office would not even accept letters coming to Rwanda. Electricity was off and on continuously. Where do we start?"

Ben adds, "Our job was to help rebuild a church that had only begun a few years earlier. It had several hundred members. Only nine have survived. The leadership has been decimated. The people are traumatized."

Darlene concludes with, "Together we cried out to God for His help. Then that peace that can only come from our Heavenly Father came again. Fears were replaced with new courage. The task ahead is great, but God is big enough."

The electricity is still off more than it is on. They haven't found their missing furnishings, but the church is growing, and people are feeling the healing hand of the Lord.

Because of people like the Odells, Rwanda will more than survive, it will grow. It will take its place among the other nations of the world where "God's ways were not man's ways" and where "man may have meant it for evil, but God meant it for good."

The kind of missionaries needed in Rwanda are those who will put their hands to the plow and never look back.

The names of Odell, Hanson, Ferguson, and Bennett, blend graciously with Moffatt, Livingstone, Grenfell, and Slessor, as they become one with hundreds of those who have gone before, and—hopefully—are yet to come.

Narrowing Down the Problem

"Let not the wise man glory in his wisdom,
Let not the mighty man glory in his might,
Nor let the rich man glory in his riches;
But let him who glories glory in this,
That he understands and knows Me,
That I am the Lord, exercising lovingkindness, judgment, and
righteousness in the earth.
For in these I delight," says the LORD.
Jeremiah 9:23–24

If all we learn from Rwanda is an attestation of man's propensity for evil, then all the suffering will have been for naught.

The disaster in Rwanda has to be seen as more than a "sound bite" in a daily pageantry of man's determined effort to destroy himself and everyone else. It contains too many parallels, too many ironies, to be simply set on the sidewalk of history for a Friday morning recycling collection.

What has and is happening now in this small Central African nation is a microcosm of the entire continent of Africa and other nations as well.

In our brief lifetime, we have seen history repeat itself more times than we wish to enumerate. The only real variance is geographical and statistical.

The process has almost become as perfunctory as predictable.

First we hear a few innocuous words, almost as an aside, about some political "trouble spot." A brief image of bodies, followed by some statistics that have long ceased to penetrate minds desensitized to "body counts."

Our moment of discomfort is replaced by images of two rich men pulling up beside each other in their chauffeur-driven limos, asking if they can share some mustard.

The UN responds with a blizzard of meetings, press releases, apocryphal warnings. Our leaders, depending on the political climate, express "real concern."

Non-governmental and humanitarian agencies begin to rally their supporters.

A "peace-keeping mission" is dispatched.

The cycle continues as the Arafats of history stare out of the bushes with their beady little eyes, and then slither around an apple core to start the process all over again.

The frustration comes from our attempts to do more than just alleviate the present suffering. We are attempting to break this terrible cycle, to have a genuine concern for victims, who—through no fault of their own—are paying a terrible price in personal tragedy, and to help bring about a meaningful resolution so the cycle will not be repeated with even greater viciousness.

We must understand that man is inherently evil, and until such time as the perpetrator is locked away forever, we will have crusades, holocausts, Cambodias, cultural revolutions, and Rwandas. This fact should not keep us from searching for a better way to handle man's basic problems.

Rwanda may be a catalyst to cause us to think hard and long about what we can do, personally and collectively.

The cycle that really needs to be broken is not so much the killings and the mayhem, but our feeble, though well-meaning attempts to alleviate the suffering. We are often "the blind leading the blind."

The dedication of those who give their lives to help others in desperate need is worthy of praise. However, something is missing, and that is our ability to discern what the real need may be.

We need a new vision.

This is not a new problem. History is plagued with disasters that have run their courses only because there were no more victims. God cried out to His chosen people,

[You] keep on hearing, but do not understand; keep on seeing, but do not perceive. [And because you do not listen I will] make the heart of this people dull, and their ears heavy, and shut their eyes; lest they see with their eyes, and hear with their ears, and understand with their heart... (Isaiah 6:9-10).

Helen Keller, blind from infancy, was asked, "What is worse than being blind?" Her reply could not be more contemporary: "There is nothing quite so pathetic as having sight but lacking vision—having sight but not seeing."

Eyes to see, but not seeing.

Her words take us back to a time when children were being massacred, slavery was an accepted way of life, punishment was meted out in the cruelest form possible, ethnic cleansing was not just politically, but religiously correct and practiced.

One came upon the scene, looked it over, wept, and "seeing the multitudes, He had compassion."

Vision implies seeing. Seeing is more than visual contact or a disturbing statistic. The very word means to "feel others' needs like they are our own," " to feel the heat of another body," "to smell them."

Some years ago, as a young person, I watched a demonstration at the UC Berkeley campus. I forget what the cause of the moment was, but one protestation sign stuck with me. I have thought of it as I watched bodies float down the Pearl River into Hong Kong Bay; watched emaciated Cambodians falling across the border into Thailand, dying before a needle could be stuck into an elusive vein; seen Rwandans torn apart by machetes, being pushed by bulldozers into mass graves.

The words on that protester's placard remain a part of my "seeing." It read, "I taste the salt of your tears."

Whether driven by compassion or guilt we are weary of the vortex that is slowly but surely drawing us to what one recently called a "descent into hell."

What kind of vision do we need?

The same vision that Isaiah had, another man who was both puffed up with his own power and fed up with a disintegrating world.

In the year that King Uzziah died, I saw the LORD sitting on a throne, high and lifted up, and the train of His robe filled the temple. Above it stood seraphim; each one had six wings: with two he covered his face, with two he covered his feet, and with two he flew.

And one cried to another and said: "Holy, holy, holy is the LORD of hosts; The whole earth is full of His glory!"

And the posts of the door were shaken by the voice of him who cried out, and the house was filled with smoke. So I said: "Woe is me, for I am undone! Because I am a man of unclean lips, and I dwell in the midst of a people of unclean lips; for my eyes have seen the King, the LORD of hosts" (Isaiah 6:1-5).

In rather simplistic, non-theological terms, what are some of the lessons we are to learn from Rwanda and other crisis areas?

1. Isaiah's eyes were put on God, "high and lifted up." Seeing the holiness and glory of God completely changed his perspective of his nation's crisis.

2. When Isaiah saw God, he cried out, "Woe is me...I am undone." I have been looking at the problem through my own eyes. No wonder my vision is blurred. "I am undone!" Everything I was so proud of, those things I put such trust in have fallen apart. My talents, my dedication, my "compassion," my abilities, my "pure" motives, have been seen as "unclean." I thought I was collecting jewels for a crown, but I am really little more than a garbage collector!

There is nothing quite so sad as having sight but lacking vision—having sight but not seeing.

We now see that our responsibility is not to solve all the problems of the world, *but to see God,* to be reminded that they are His problems, and if we want to participate in solving them we must see them through His eyes. But first, we must see Him.

It will make a difference when someone looks us in the face and spits out the question, "Where was that God of yours when those young hoodlums killed my family?" We can reply, tearfully and humbly, "He was in the same place as the day hoodlums like you and me nailed His only Son to a cross. He was there, high and lifted up, with out-stretched arms. Stretched out not to rescue His son from our wickedness, but to hold back His armies of angels until in the fullness of time He could redeem our wicked-ness. God is not concerned with only a temporary rescue from suffering, but with eternal redemption."

To first see God, and then see the world as He sees it, brings into focus what G. Campbell Morgan talked about in his book *The Crisis of the Christ*,[1] and gives us some needed insight. He says,

In all the works of God there is to be discovered an unvarying method of process and crisis. The process is slow [five hundred years in Rwanda] and difficult to watch. The process suddenly burst upon us [like a plane going down in flames] and we have a crisis.

The crisis is sudden, and flames with a light, which, flashing back upon the process, explains it, and indicates a new line of actions; the continuity of that has preceded it.

A crisis is not an accident, not a catastrophe, in the sense of disaster, but a stage in an orderly method.

Campbell goes on to point out that this is graphically illustrated in the life of Christ, which records a continu-ous process and seven crises. First, the crisis of His birth, then baptism, temptation, transfiguration, crucifixion, resurrection, and finally, the ascension. "Each of these crises ushered in a new order of things in the work of Christ, crowning that of the past and creating the force for that which was to come."

Basically then, a "crisis" is part of God's plan to help us grow, and to be an integral part of His plan for the ages.

So what happens? Simple. A crisis comes along and because we have not seen God and the crisis from His point of view, we attempt to infuse our plans, our intellect, and our wisdom into the situation.

Now we no longer have a *crisis*. We have a *disaster*.

By simple definition, a "crisis" is part and parcel of God's plan for His universe. A "disaster" is what results when we take that crisis and try to solve it with our limited wisdom, intellect, and expertise.

Welcome to Rwanda!

This new crisis-cum-disaster is not unique. Enmity has displayed itself under many names. It is being enacted each day in such familiar places as the West Bank, Golan Heights, and Bethlehem, where the crisis of our Lord's mother-to-be first was met with a stop-them-in-their-tracks epiphany.

U.S. Ambassador to Rwanda David Rawson, son of a medical doctor in Burundi, places Rwanda's crisis in proper perspective, comparing it with a situation the apostle Paul refers to in the book of Ephesians.

[This crisis] outlines a deep division in civil society based on differences in history, culture and religion. The Jewish people traced their history back to Abraham; they were by birth participants in an historic covenant relationship between God and Abraham that made them God's special people, inheritors of a promised redemption through the Messiah/Christ. They wrapped that understanding of themselves and their role in the world in daily habits and rituals, religious observances and communal festivals as outlined in the Law, the Torah. Each male in Israel bore in his body a symbolic reminder of his obligations to the law, to the covenant and to God—he was circumcised eight days after his birth.

On the other side of the division were Gentiles—everybody who was not Jewish.... They were of Greco-Roman culture, had tired of their own humanistic gods, longed for worship of one true God and for a sense of history and of purpose that would bring meaning to their frenetic lives in one of the Roman empire's busiest port cities. They had Jewish neighbors whom they envied for their determined faith and fervent practice. But these Gentiles were kept away from all that. They were not born Jewish, they had no access to the Covenant, nor to the Messianic promise. Paul brutally reminds the Ephesian Gentiles in chapter 2:12 that they were separate from the Messiah, excluded from citizenship in Israel, foreigners to the covenant of promise, without hope and without God in the world. What kept these two groups apart Paul called the great barrier, the dividing wall of hostility, that is—"the law with its commandments and regulations." All that defined Jewish identity: their daily rituals, acts of worship, festival observances kept the Gentiles from experiencing the heart of Jewish vocation in the world, a covenant relationship with God. And this would never change—he would always be derided as "uncircumcised" by those that called themselves "circumcised."

Ambassador Rawson then switches centuries and continents and explains the parallel with Rwanda's deep division of their society, and goes on to conclude:

This slaughter of innocents makes us shudder, because we intuitively sense that the ways we have identified ourselves as distinct from others, the laws, customs, etiquettes that make us feel at ease with ourselves, comfortable and superior to our neighbors are the building blocks of those walls of hostility that can encompass killing fields. That is the bad news.

The good news is that Christ, in the words of Ephesians 2:14 can still make the two one and has "broken down the barrier, the dividing wall of hostility." Having witnessed the early phases of this decade's worst killings, I confess that I do not begin to understand how this can be so, but by faith I take it as good news that:

God crossed the great divide between Himself and man, shared in human suffering and thus made it possible for us to get beyond all that defines our lives: the customs, habits, and pretensions which separate us from others. Paul says Christ was "abolishing in his flesh the law with its commandments and regulations."

In identifying with the depth of human suffering which Christ endured on the cross, we too can somehow bridge the growing sense of difference between us and others, difference that breeds hostility and can produce genocide. Paul says Christ "put to death their hostility through the cross." At the cross and in the face of human suffering, our superiority, our status or our grievances fall away.

Christ's purpose in coming to the world was to make peace between hostile persons, to put them in right relationship with each other and with God. "His purpose was to make one new man out of the two, thus making peace and to reconcile both of them to God through the cross."

This message of peace and this process of reconciliation to each other and to God opens the way to God for all men. "We all have access to the Father through the spirit," the barriers between us crumble—we can accept our former enemy as a fellow citizen with God's people and member of God's household.

The bad news is that the walls of difference, hostility and hatred are still there between Jew and Gentile, between Anglo and Hispanic, between Serb and Bosnian, between Hutu and Tutsi. Human suffering and dehumanizing conflict grows apace. Genocide still happens.

The Gospel's good news is that when we accept our common humanity, when we understand that God has, in Christ, shared our suffering, and when we believe that the way to God is open to all of us despite our differences, then we become open to reconciliation with those we had despised and can welcome Christ's peace which sets all things right.

In Ephesians 2:17, Paul quotes a prophecy. Let me give you the full rendition from Isaiah 57: "I have seen his ways but I will heal him, I will guide him and restore comfort to him, creating praise on the lips of mourners from Israel. Peace, peace to those far and near," says the Lord, "And I will heal them." I claim that promise today for Hutu and Tutsi in Rwanda and for myself.

Not withstanding the Ambassador's wisdom, we still have a crisis-cum-disaster that needs to be resolved. We can do one of several things:

- ignore the past and reinvent the wheel;

- maintain the way things have always been done, ignoring the dictum that "the past is a wonderful teacher, but a lousy roommate";

- take all we know about process and crisis, see God high and lifted up and let God give us His vision.

1 G. Campbell Morgan, *The Crisis of the Christ* (Fleming H. Revell Company, 1936), 16–17.

Discipleship —the Cost

My heart within me is broken
Because of the prophets;
All my bones shake.
I am like a drunken man,
And like a man whom wine has overcome,
Because of the LORD,
And because of His holy words
(Jeremiah 23:9).

Rwanda is pregnant with lessons to be brought forth. The most demanding of attention is the cost to followers of Jesus.

Someone wrote: "He who has not suffered has not lived." This philosophy is diametrically opposed to our society's, which holds that we have more rights than responsibilities; that God is a God of love who only wants us to be happy and that it blesses Him to supply all our material, spiritual, and physical needs—all we have to do is ask. Some think of Him as a "Cadillac God who wants all His children to have a Cadillac."

What a farce this makes of the whole concept of there being a cost to being a disciple of Jesus Christ.

Aleksandr Solzhenitsyn, one of our few modern prophets (that we stoned by our silence), described in his book *The Gulag Archipelago*,[1] how one finds true Christianity.

> It was in my prison camp that for the first time I understood reality. It was there that I realized that the line between good and evil passes not between countries, not between political parties, not between classes, but down, straight down each separate individual human heart....

> It was on rotting straw in my labor camp that I learned this and I thank you, prison, for teaching me this truth.... Bless you, prison, for having been in my life.

Compare this with our minimum standards of Christian culture.

In a speech Solzhenitsyn made this reference to lessons learned in a prison cell:

> In agonizing moments in camps, in columns of prisoners at night, in the freezing darkness through which the lanterns shone, there often arose in our throats something we wanted to shout out to the whole world, if only the world could have heard one of us. Such ideas come not from books and were not borrowed for the sake of harmony or coherence. They were formulated in prison cells and around forest campfires, in conversations with persons now dead, were hardened by that life developed out there.

"Bless you, prison, for having been in my life."

Christian discipleship, a commitment to responding to hate and injustice as Jesus responded, following Jesus' example and learning of Him, is a costly business. Salvation is a free gift, but living it out has its cost.

Too many of us want the Christmas experience, being born anew, and then we want to move right to Pentecost, where we assume the action is. We have made discipleship a game in which we roll the dice and draw a card, hoping it will say, "Go directly to Pentecost, do not stop at go."

What about the forty days and nights of standing toe to toe with the devil himself? What about the nights in prayer, crying out, *Oh, Father, won't these guys ever learn? I think they are about ready, but, well you saw what they did today?*

We must spend time supping with Him and feeling His heartache at our bickering. We must identify with our part in His betrayal.

He was surrounded by a sleeping church, including the chosen three (the pastoral staff). "They have told me so many times how much they love me and that I am their leader, but listen to their snoring." In our mind's eye we must see what Jesus saw—the Garden's olive press. He knew its purpose—to strip the olives and crush their flesh and seed so the oil would flow. We must enter into His willingness to be like the olives for His holy oil is needed for anointing, not only those who fall asleep, but for those who cry out for deliverance from no sleep.

"Not my will but Thine be done," is the willingness to sacrifice one's life for the sake of another, the ultimate mark of a disciple of Jesus. Will we follow His example?

"Into Your hands I commit My Spirit...all I am, all I

want to be, all I want to do."

Rwanda's salvation and healing can only come through the process of evangelism *and* discipleship, submitting to "Not my will but Thine be done," realizing there are no short cuts to Pentecost.

1 Aleksandr I. Solzhenitsyn, *The Gulag Archipelago*, 2 (Harper and Row), 615.

Healing and Revival

"I will restore health to you,
and heal you of your wounds," says the LORD
(Jeremiah 30:17).

Rwanda's wounds are deep. Much healing will need to take place before forgiveness and reconciliation are possible. As we see the souls of the wounded, we realize Rwanda is like an overwhelmed hospital ward, where well-meaning workers are applying bandages and handing out pain killers, but where a great physician is desperately needed in order to bring healing.

Look closely at the sufferers.

There is a Tutsi soldier who went into exile with his father as a child, and now is back as part of the RPF. His sickness is out of control, vengeance runs through his veins. He recounts in graphic detail how twenty years ago the Hutus crucified his father—they stuck him in an African ant hill and made the family watch as he was slowly eaten alive.

Notice the young Hutu soldier sitting in a refuge camp. He is filled with self-loathing, unable to turn off his mind's replay of his part in the savagery.

Jon Sommers walked through one of those camps and saw the despair in the eyes of many like this soldier. He attempts to give voice to their silent hopelessness.

I saw death...I caused death. I killed. I murdered. I took the lives of the children He loves. I raped the women in front of their husbands and then mercilessly slaughtered them all. Was that me? Did I really do that? Yes, I did. I remember it barely, like through a haze. But I remember the faces, dear God, I remember the faces. It's one thing to kill with a gun in a war, another to keep hacking until the silence of death comes. It wasn't me, was it? I live with a murderer—myself. Do you think that's easy? Death would be a pleasant escape. Really, I am more dead than my victims. Their bodies are dead and rotted, but my soul is dead and darkened beyond hope. There is no hope for me. A god, if there is one, could never love me. Now, the time has come to go. I leave nothing but hate and grief. What have I done to the children?... This world needs to be rid of me. One more death won't matter. Please don't hate me—I already hate myself enough. Please, the hell of what I have done is enough hell for me. Please forgive me...please? No matter, I am leaving. All is dark....

Wandering here somewhere is a teen-age girl, tortured by the memory of a choice she was forced to make. She was sixteen, maybe seventeen, married and nine months pregnant when the Hutus came and the slaughter contin-ued. Her husband disappeared. Later, she found out he had been killed. When she saw her mother and father were dead she escaped and ran for the bushes.

She joined up with two other young girls as they made a desperate trek across the hills. Heavy with child, she was barely able to walk, let alone keep up. Finally, the river was in sight. Seeing the camp and safety were in reach, she sat down to rest when the labor pains began. Her friends helped her to lay down and together they brought the child into the world. What now? She barely knew how to swim. How could she carry her baby to safety with her? There was a discussion and then a decision. The baby, less than an hour old, was bundled up in the moth-er's scarf and reluctantly left on the shore as the mother stepped into the water. Blood rose to the surface, spread out, and disappeared. The mother took one excruciating look back, and then weakly stretched one arm toward the opposite shore. She will live that moment of her life over and over again. Not the pangs of birth, but the moment when she had to make that painful decision—stay with the child and perhaps get captured, try to swim and both drown, or swim by herself and hope some good Samaritan would care for her baby.

These cases are multiplied many times over. Only a High Priest or a Great Physician or a Wonderful Counselor can bring health and wholeness to people in such critical condition.

How about in a narrow dormitory room in Kigali?

A metal bunk-bed frame stood alone against one wall, emphasizing the room's starkness. Against the opposite wall two small cots with mismatched spreads had been pushed together, one cot higher than the other. Only the computer on a folding card table established our setting as belong to the 1990s.

Sitting on one side of each bed were Peter and Elizabeth Guilleband, tall and slight of build like so many of their ancestors. Their faces were road maps of years of living, but gracefully aged by their countenance of peace. Her gray hair rested in a small, hastily prepared bun on top of her head. Over his face fell long white locks which he brushed aside with his veined hands as he spoke.

When they spoke, one's tone matched the other, their words were a quiet blend of gentility and conviction, washed in kindness.

Peter had come to Rwanda from his native England in 1937, Elizabeth in 1939. In 1940 they married and now, after fifty-four years together, they spoke as one, of past revivals and of their hope for another yet to come.

While they talked, I had to lift my eyes from my notepad to tell which was speaking. There was not an interruption as their thoughts and words, like their voices, blended together as one.

Peter told of his coming as a missionary while the great revival of the '30s was already in progress.

"It started in a girls' school, and before long the girls had gossiped the gospel into other schools, homes, and finally, the churches."

"Yes indeed, and of all different denominations."

"Quite so, but it made me very uncomfortable. I had never seen anything like this before, I had doubts. I was very confused and critical."

"He thought they were getting a bit emotional."

"Then one day I was visiting with a local pastor who

had befriended me. His favorite verse was 1 John 1:6. Every time he would mention it, he would repeat it as though I, a Bible student and missionary, didn't know what it said. He would smile as he'd recite, 'If we say that we have fellowship with Him, and walk in darkness, we lie and do not practice the truth.' "

"I was very upset and shouted at him, 'I know that verse. You don't have to repeat it.' But he was very loving and kind to me. One day, though I sensed there was grief in his voice, he fairly shouted, 'Peter, you are as useless to God as a crate of ammunition without a gun!' "

"That did it!"

"Yes, it surely did. I was convinced I needed to come to the cross. That He could not use me unless I would allow Him to help Himself to all of me. And so I made that decision...I went to the cross. I wasn't sure I had ever really been there before."

Both of them were silent for a few moments, and then, "And He is still working in me today. I find myself going daily to the cross for more of Him."

"And I was just as bad as Peter. There was much talk back home about a 'spiritual experience.' I didn't understand it, but I knew I wanted it. Then one day I realized that my problem was that I was looking for an experience and what I really needed was a Person."

They touched each other's hands across the bed, smiled, and continued.

"Our dear friend, Roy Hession had asked us, 'Peter, Elizabeth, are you candidates for His grace, weak and empty, with nothing in the tank?' "

"We experienced the wonderful revival of the '30s which went well into the '40s, and then began to cool."

"Yes, what a tragedy, to lose something so precious."

"We went back to England, and then God brought us back here in the '70s."

"It was to this very place."

"Even today, we are not sure why we are here. Then, as now, we feel a bit helpless."

"Feeling helpless, at least we weren't a hindrance to the revival that was then beginning to flame up again here in Rwanda."

"Interesting, that as in the '30s, it began in a girls' school."

"Yes, missionary Mabel Jones..."

"What a beautiful lady..."

"She was a teacher in a French-speaking girls' school."

"Mabel told us that though the girls lived together and tolerated each other, there was no fellowship, no real love. I remembered, 'You are as useless to God as a crate of ammunition without a gun.'"

"Then, one day, while praying in one of Mabel's classes, a young girl began to weep. The students got very nervous, but they sensed that God was there. After a time, she stood before the students and confessed to them that she was guilty of two great sins."

"This had never happened before, even though it was a Christian school."

"Her two sins were of course, the sins of them all: tribalism and cheating in her schoolwork—dishonesty."

"The dam broke, didn't it?"

"Yes, this young girl came to the cross. All revival begins seemingly, from a crisis, like Calvary."

"Soon, instead of classes there were prayer meetings. It was not only the girls who were affected but the leadership of the school as well."

"Girls would go off alone with only a Bible and hymnal. You would hear them praying and singing, often crying and speaking aloud to God, repenting. It was a sound that would continue at night as the girls lay under their blankets in the dormitories, dormitories just like this."

"Remember? There was the Muslim lady who heard about what was happening and came to the school to see what it was that was changing these girls' lives."

"Yes, the nice thing about girls is they have to talk. They, too, gossiped the gospel everywhere they went."

"They went to the boys' schools, then to the churches. Everywhere they went the results were the same. Their message was always simple, but always there were tears, repentance, and reconciliation."

"It was a wonderful time for us as well. Denominationalism was set aside."

"Yes, all the people wanted to talk about was Jesus Christ. We didn't much care any longer about Calvinism or Armenianism, Sanctification, Pentecostalism..."

"Now we just talked about the Lord, what He meant to us and how He was changing our lives."

"We were already in our late sixties and retired, so we returned once again to England."

"Then, just a short time ago, in early 1994, we began getting letters from our Rwandan friends telling us of difficult times. They sensed something terrible was certain to happen. The animosity between the Hutus and Tutsis was boiling over."

"One friend wrote and said that she had had a vision of blood flowing in her country. She said she saw many chariots going to heaven loaded with people."

"So, again, here we are. We feel helpless. I don't know why we are here, but we know this is where God wants us."

"We believe that where the fires of revival once burned they will burn again, as they did in the Welsh revival during both World War I and World War II.

"Yes, yes, revival follows Calvary."

"Already we see the fires beginning to burn."

"Yes indeed, what else would enable a dear friend of ours, faced again and again by Hutu soldiers ready to kill her, to calmly say, 'You can kill me if you like, but you will then be alone with your sins, and the sin of killing me as well. What will you do about that?' The soldiers put down their weapons and walked away. She would say to each one who meant to kill her, 'Before you kill me, may I ask you a question? Are you saved?'"

There was resolution in their voices as they continued.

"But now that part is over, and we must get on with the business at hand. We must forget about who did what to whom, and begin to deal with our own personal sins."

"Yes, as we did in the '30s. We did not deal with the injustices against us, but with our own injustice against our Lord, our greed, our own lust, our own lack of brokenness."

Standing, an unspoken signal that the interview was nearly over, "I told you I came here searching for a 'spiritual experience.' Someone gave me five steps to revival...no, don't write them down—they mean nothing. I have found out there is only one step to revival. Step right across everything else, and hurry as fast as you can to the feet of Jesus at Calvary."

Peter could not walk all the way to the door. He was still suffering the effects of a recent stroke. As they said goodbye, they spoke the same words, separately, and then in unison, "Yes, yes, we must be specific about our sin."

When General Booth died, it seemed The Salvation Army might die with him. Booth's successor, Sam Brengle, stood looking out over London, seeing drunks and hooligans, living out their sin on the same streets on which the Salvationists used to preach and sing, and he cried out, "Lord, You did it once. Do it again."

That must be our cry for Rwanda.

"Through the Lord's mercies we are not consumed, because His compassions fail not. They are new every morning; Great is Your faithfulness. 'The Lord is my portion,' says my soul, 'Therefore I hope in Him!' " (Lamentations 3:22–24).

...Light

One can not just walk away from Rwanda without feeling some very strong and lasting emotions.

You think of the tiny babies that were torn from their mothers' breasts just before the mothers were hacked to death. Rwanda is not unlike those tiny infants, left to die but mercifully rescued, at least for the present, by strangers.

That determined smile on the faces of those attempting to rebuild their lives is closer to being a stifled groan. They are like many of the buildings whose bullet holes have been plastered over, but the splotches of mismatched paint remind you that inside, the scars are still there, unhealed, undealt with, liable to fester into revenge before they can heal through reconciliation.

Rwanda remains a nation of darkness and fear. Fear that one day, while in the marketplace or riding a bus or standing on a street corner, someone will yell, "That's him, that's the one who killed my children. Arrest him!"

And vigilante justice will place them in a crowded jail cell, where they could spend years before being brought to "justice."

It is also a country of hope and light.

Missionary Ron Hanson and his passenger are making their way through the morning marketplace traffic. Kigali is slowly coming to life as Land Rovers, UN vehicles, and some private cars attempt to navigate without the help of street lights. The passenger's husband has returned, and their children are safe in Zaire, but she still feels sadness that her best friend, with her two little girls, is still missing.

In the middle of a conversation, Ron slams on his brakes when his passenger screams. "It's her! It's her! She's alive!" She is instantly out of the Land Rover and dodging traffic, running across the road.

Ron sits and watches as Uweri and Kayitesi, who have not seen each other since they last parted at the restaurant, dance in a circle, crying, "You're alive, you're alive," and rays of light and hope return to Rwanda.

"Thus says the Lord: 'Stand in the ways and see, and ask for the old paths, where the good way is, and walk in it; Then you will find rest for your souls...'" (Jeremiah 6:16).

Afterword

The words of longshoreman philosopher, Eric Hoffer[1], though penned in the late seventies, aptly describe Rwanda. He wrote: "The belly of the world has been ripped open and we see what we hoped we would never have to see."

But standing as we do in the middle of the white line on the great communication-cybernetic highway, we have seen it whether we wanted to or not. The question is, what can we do about it?

Several recommendations:

1. Support Christian relief organizations. Nothing in this book should be construed as criticism of the non-governmental organizations and the work they have done and continue to do for Rwanda. There may be one or two that misuse your generosity, but God will honor your motive for giving,

2. Missions works—don't stop now.

3. When you see the name, Rwanda, in the newspaper

or hear the name on the evening news, let that be a prayer reminder. Jesus does not say, "if you pray," but "when you pray." Intercessory prayer is to be an unconditioned reflex, like breathing. As our suffering brothers and sisters are brought to our attention, breathe prayer for them.

3. Alexis de Tocqueville said, "Whoever is not called upon to struggle is forgotten by God." Rwanda has not been forgotten. Neither have we. Our struggle may not be what we have seen in the preceding pages, but more like Jacob's as he wrestled with the Lord. Consider setting aside twenty-four hours for a time of wrestling, praying, and fasting for Rwanda.

I was introduced to the power of intercessory prayer when at the very beginning of Glasnost I interviewed a young Russian dissident in Moscow, freed for a special meeting with visiting President Ronald Reagan. Alex Ogorodnikov had been sent to Siberia for having Bible studies in his home. While in prison, people from Brother Andrew's group smuggled in a letter telling him there was a prayer chain praying for him twenty-four hours a day. He then smuggled this letter out to Brother Andrew.

He began by quoting 2 Corinthians 4:9, "We are persecuted, but not forsaken..."

> I bow my head and bend my knee in deepest gratitude for your prayers and compassionate activity in defense of your Russian fellow-Christians.

> It is in the concentration camps which are scattered over the vast expanse of Russia, behind tall fences of barbed wire and high voltage cables, to the accompaniment of the frenzied howling of guard dogs, as you are buried in the tomb-like twilight of solitary punishment cells, when the oppressive

silence of faceless days turns time itself into an instrument of torture, when the heart begins to fail and your tongue cleaves to the roof of your mouth in a senseless babble of misery, when hunger gnaws your belly, the cold numbs your flesh and desperation courses through your blood—then, it seems that an indifferent world has already consigned you to the grave, that the scrap of sky visible through the small window grating has closed over you, that you feel totally alone and abandoned, and despair washes over you like a tide.

But it was in these terrible moments in icy cells that I physically felt the warmth of your prayers and compassion, a force linking us by a stream of spiritual energy generated by mutual experience of faith and the mysterious bonds of fraternal unity.

It was like the warm touch of a brotherly hand, which had moved aside the strands of barbed wire and penetrated through gloomy walls. The strength of your love and compassion turned my despair into indestructible hope, my cries into prayers, and the edge of madness into enlightenment.

Your intercession for persecuted Christians and all prisoners of conscience awakens the moral consciousness of the world before the face of hatred, bears witness to the dignity and value of every living being as the image and likeness of God. It is living confirmation of the unity of the mother-church, and brings us to the realization of the truth that we are all members of the body of Christ, and if one member feels pain, then the whole body suffers. In your selfless defense of the faith against the forces of evil, you have given a selfish world an impressive object lesson in love, and in compassion and unity, and the all-seeing God heard your prayer, accepted your sacrifice, and paid heed to your voice of witness and denunciation of the persecutors. He opened the doors of the dungeons, and set the prisoners free. Se we are living witnesses of how your love, faith and deeds are changing the course of history. In addressing these inadequate words of thanks to you for your concern with our bonds, I am painfully aware of my inability to express the extent of the gratitude which filled my heart toward you during the long ninety-nine months of my imprisonment.

May the Lord sustain you in your great task of intercession for the persecuted, the humiliated and the oppressed. May your voice never be silenced before the face of the persecutors, a voice which bears witness to our Savior Jesus Christ, a voice which defends the persecuted from the attempts of evil to seize souls and vanquish freedom, and which stirs an indifferent world to compassion for the driven."

1 Hoffer, Eric, *Before The Sabbath*, (Harper and Row) 1979

RWANDAN REFUGEES

Full of terror these people run
 seeking refuge, anywhere
Behind them, lifeless bodies lie
 does our world really care?

Little kids who've watched the horror
 orphaned now, sit and stare
At night they reach with trembling hands
 but find no love or care.

Hungry, broken, with no tomorrow
 their fate just isn't fair
And our world looks the other way
 its wealth too dear to share.

How can five hundred thousand die
 with only vultures there?
How can we just switch the channel?
 Why...why do so few care?

And now, dear Heavenly Father
 please hear my humble prayer
Give all of us your loving heart
 and teach us how to share.

 —Jim Grams
 May 18, 1994

AFRICA

Look just beyond the runway
    out past the waiting plane,
Grasses tall and endless
    a brown and long terrain.

You almost wait for lions
    or men with spears and shields,
But they're all gone away now
    just like the fertile fields.

We are lifting from the runway
    below, just grass and shrubs,
Africa no longer is a place
    where wars are fought with clubs.

It weeps with blood and hatred
    as guns scream in the night,
Fathers no longer tell their sons
    that all will come out right.

Stomachs empty, fields bare
    the sun as hot as ever,
Hope is gone, and peace?
    not here, not now, not never!

Unless Africans hear God's truth
    Real peace they'll never know,
We are Christ's love and peace to them
    And that is why we go.

    —Jim Grams
    Guinea Bissau airport 2/94

THEIR EYES, LORD

I have seen those beautiful dark brown eyes,
    Seen them sparkle with Joy and wonder.
But Lord, I need to talk to you about some troubled eyes,
    The ones I often see when mine are closed.

Please help me to do more, I'm sure I can,
    Don't ever let me forget those haunting, hurting eyes.
Help me change their eyes of fear to ones that trust,
    And give those empty, hungry eyes, the sight of real food.

Give me a way to pierce the stares of AIDS' tiny ones,
    so they can watch with me a glimpse of Heaven.
Bright beautiful eyes at birth, now dimmed and lifeless,
    I must reach them Lord, with You, their only hope.

Some stare into emptiness, and some just glare with hatred,
    Their eyes, Lord, surely search for you.
Yet all they see around them is hunger, horror and death,
    When they see me, dear Jesus, please let them see you.

Somehow, my Lord, I must do more, I must, I MUST!
    Africa's children can no longer wait,
Tomorrow is not nearly good enough,
    I hope and pray I'm not already late.

Their eyes, Lord, don't ever let me forget their eyes.

    Their Eyes, Lord...Jim Grams Jan 17, 1994

THE CHILDREN ARE DYING

Landmines, cholera, stalvation, guns
  You may take your pick
Africa's children keep on dying
  Death comes far too quick

AIDS horrors come attacking
  Deep inside the womb
And precious infants entering life
  Go quickly to their tomb

They stand in lines of refugees
  Without dad, or mom
Suddenly life is blown apart
  Victims of a bomb

A cup of clear cold water
  Isn't very much
But to a dying helpless child
  Brings a loving touch

The world keeps on rushing by
  With no more than a shrug
But those who follow Jesus
  Bend down, to give a hug

One day we'll stand at heaven's gate
  With children we have won
And hear our Lord and Saviour say
  Enter now, well done

    —Jim Grams 11/94

HELP FOR AFRICA

I'm circling one more little airport
    with Africa down below,
A place where life's a struggle
    and most everything moves slow.

I wonder, as I breathe a prayer
    for those who live down there,
Why millions who have plenty
    for these don't really care.

It's easier just to close our eyes
    pretending all is well,
Yet seeing Africa today
    s' like looking into hell.

Hunger, hatred, disease and death
    are rampant in the bush,
Economies just keep on dying
    as powers pull and push.

And what about the children
    whose suffering is the worst,
Three hundred million strong
    we need to place them first.

If we who have, do nothing
    but watch the children cry,
If we won't love, give or care
    this Afriea will die.

The children aren't the ones at fault
    for hope they sit and wait,
Let's give them love and Jesus Christ
    before it is too late.

    —Jim Grams
    On a plans to Africa 2/94